Public Expressions of Religion in America

Conrad Cherry, *Series Editor*

Published in cooperation with the
Center for the Study of Religion and American Culture
Indiana University–Purdue University at Indianapolis

Producing the Sacred

Producing the Sacred

An Essay on Public Religion

Robert Wuthnow

University of Illinois Press
Urbana and Chicago

© 1994 by the Board of Trustees of the University of Illinois
Manufactured in the United States of America
1   2   3   4   5   C   P   5   4   3   2   1

This book is printed on acid-free paper.

Library of Congress Cataloging-in-Publication Data

Wuthnow, Robert.
    Producing the sacred : an essay on public religion / Robert
Wuthnow.
        p.   cm. — (Public expressions of religion in America)
    ISBN 0-252-01920-2 (cl. : alk. paper). — ISBN 0-252-06401-1
    (pb. : alk. paper)
    1. United States — Religion — 1960–   I. Title.   II. Series.
BL2525.W879   1994
306.6'0973 — dc20   93-8934
                                                            CIP

Contents

Acknowledgments

I especially thank Conrad Cherry, director of the Project on Public Religion from which this volume grew, and the Lilly Endowment for its sponsorship of this project. In addition to the various project meetings and symposia made possible by that project, I have benefited from conversations with a wide variety of religious leaders and scholars, from the opportunity to participate in the activities of a number of religious organizations, and from my own funded research on related aspects of religion in American life. At the risk of forgetting some of the individuals whose remarks have especially shaped my ideas about public religion and at the risk of embarrassing others, I acknowledge my gratitude to Gene Burns, professor of sociology at Princeton University; James Turner, professor of history at the University of Michigan; Roy Rappaport, professor of anthropology at the University of Michigan; Edward Dohey, professor emeritus at Princeton Theological Seminary; George Gallup, Jr., president of the George H. Gallup International Institute; Thomas Gillispie, president of Princeton Theological Seminary; Virginia Hodgkinson of Independent Sector, Inc.; Lonnie H. Lee, pastor of John Knox Presbyterian Church in Tulsa; John Mulder, president of Louisville Presbyterian Theological Seminary; and Nicholas Van Dyck, president of Religion in American Life. I also thank those at the following organizations who organized conferences, arranged meetings, or shared information with me about various kinds of religious organizations: the Association for Religion and Intellectual Life, the Center for Ethics and Public Policy, the Fundamentalism Project at the University of Chicago, the Institute for Church and State Studies

at Baylor University, Interfaith Impact, the Presbyterian Church
U.S.A., Religion in American Life, the Russell Sage Foundation, and
Vesper International. Several reporters whose names I have lost track
of were helpful in discussing various aspects of public religion with
me, and structured interviews conducted with several local clergy,
whose names will be kept confidential, were useful in providing insights into the activities of local congregations. I thank Natalie Searl
for conducting and transcribing these interviews. Help in formulat-
ing the ideas presented here also came from the numerous colleagues
and students with whom I worked on my project on religion and
the voluntary sector, from discussions sponsored by the Center for
Human Values at Princeton University, and from my associates at
the Center for the Study of American Religion at Princeton University, particularly Albert J. Raboteau and John F. Wilson.

Introduction

The title of this essay—*Producing the Sacred*—is deliberately contentious. What could be more spontaneous, more completely beyond our control, than the sacred? How can it possibly be "produced"?

The sacred comes to us, tradition says, as a revelation of the numinous, an epiphany, a gift of grace. God spoke to Moses through the burning bush, not because Moses had done something to evoke the sacred but simply because God chose to do so. The dove representing the holy spirit that descended on Jesus as he was being baptized in Galilee had not first risen as a prayer of entreaty to God; it simply descended. How then can the sacred be produced?

Suggesting that it may be produced is contentious not simply because it differs from tradition but also because it still seems to take something away from the sacred to think of it this way. Unless we are dogmatic fundamentalist bashers, we prefer not to think that the early Christians got together and "made up" the New Testament. Hearing television preachers announce they have had a revelation from God, we may be cynical, but we would prefer to think they really had (sincerely) been in communion with the divine. We prefer to think people's experiences of the sacred in their ordinary lives are not merely the result of overexhaustion or pharmaceuticals.

Yet we know that much of what we call religion is indeed produced. Try as they might to seem spontaneous in the pulpit, the local preachers have probably spent long hours during the preceding week preparing their remarks. The very fact that there is a pulpit at all means someone at some point paid the mortgage and the utility bill, and before that someone passed the plate, and people put in their offerings to hire an architect to design a building and pay a contractor to build it. Most expressions of modern religion are like this. Pastors are trained to be in contact with the sacred, meetinghouses are constructed to provide a place for gods to dwell, publishing companies print and distribute the Bibles we read, even our private meditations may be performed with a background of recorded music. We have come to expect this because it is no different from the rest of our lives. Everything we do is deeply dependent on the efforts and resources supplied by someone.

The problem, though, is that religion and the sacred are not the same thing. It may seem right to argue that religion is produced, for religion is always a matter of institutions and organizations and professional roles and finances. It seems less correct to say the sacred is produced because that still connotes something more basic, either a transcendent being that exists despite any human efforts or a deeply subjective experience that also cannot be manipulated into existence. In insisting that the sacred itself may be produced, therefore, I am suggesting something intentionally more difficult to resolve than to say only that religion is produced.

Here I must make a confession, however. Being a social scientist and making the statement I have just made, I make myself vulnerable to the accusation that old-style, nineteenth-century positivist reductionism has again raised its ugly head. When the founders of modern social science said the sacred was produced, they meant it quite literally. Marx thought there was nothing beyond the skies that had not been placed there by the projections of greedy capitalists seeking to legitimate themselves. In the later and more sober reflections of Émile Durkheim, much the same view is present: primitives made up stories about the gods and paid ritual obeisance to them, he argued, because they felt the power of society over them and needed some way to express their awe toward this power; moderns were scarcely different, although their sense of the sacred might be attached to flags and public figures rather to than holy stones and ancestral animals. The social sciences, however, have moved well beyond these early reductionistic arguments in the past half-century. The sacred may now be regarded as a form of culture deeply conditioned by the language and the social contexts in which it appears, but the argument that "nothing exists" other than our own fantasies about the sacred is no longer credible, and I do not accept it either. In other words, it is entirely possible to talk about the sacred's being dependent on human institutions without staking out theological claims that would either deny or affirm the possibility of the sacred's acting independently of (or upon) these institutions.

When I assert that the sacred is produced, therefore, I do so to orient our thinking toward two critical issues: first, individuals, communities, and organizations are indeed in some ways responsible for the continuing existence of the sacred in our society; and second, it is not just religion about which we must ask, especially if religion is regarded as a bland, gray-suited creature already, but also the sacred, that is, the symbolic frameworks that are set apart from everyday life, giving a sense of transcendent, holistic meaning. Both issues are terribly important to consider, and perhaps even arrive at a better understanding of, because the health of society itself depends on how we understand them. Were the sacred to disappear from our lives, we would surely be lessened, even in our humanity. Should the communities and organizations that have long sustained the sacred sink into nothingness, not to be replaced by other communities and organizations, the sacred would indeed be exceedingly difficult to discover.

In considering these issues, we should of course recognize how much they pertain to matters in our personal lives. Except for the small number of people who somehow live with no sense of the sacred, the questions of how to think about the sacred, where to find it, and in what manner to address it remain deeply significant. Life is, as we say, deepened and enriched by our individual experiences of the sacred. They provide us with reference points, both emotionally and intellectually, telling us that our lives have meaning and purpose. These individual experiences, however, do not exhaust the importance of the sacred. It is also, as I have deliberately asserted, crucial to the health of society. A nation cannot long exist without conceptions of the transcendent to guide its destiny and sanction its highest values. No less can a community of nations seek peace and justice, or live in harmony with the planet, without a similar conception of what is good and right and worthy of our deepest respect. This is why, in addition to whatever merit it may have for the quality of our private lives, the sacred must also be considered in its public manifestations.

The Public Expression of the Sacred

In recent years much attention has been drawn to the ways in which the sacred interacts with public life, especially through the public role of religion. Preachers' using cable television to beam their sermons across the nation, lobbyists' representing their denominations' interests on Capitol Hill, congregations' sponsoring forums on issues of community concern, and religious writers' addressing the nation's ills are but a few examples of the ways in which public religion is currently expressed. The issues vary from one place or time to another, but one thing remains constant: it takes organized effort to engage the sacred in dialogue with issues of public concern.

To say this seems so obvious on the surface. What does it mean, though, to say that organized effort is involved? Generally we think in relatively vague terms about this question, reflecting as we sometimes do on "religious interests" in American politics or on the relations between "church and state." Sometimes our references are much more specific, perhaps mentioning that "the Presbyterian church" issued a statement about human sexuality or that Pastor X was trying to turn out the vote. Still, questions arise. Just what part of the vastly complex entity we call the Presbyterian church are we referring to? Was Pastor X acting completely as a private individual, or was there some organization behind the pastor?

Social scientists have begun to contribute some helpful discussions of these matters. Electoral and public opinion research has begun to show how the adherents of various faiths and denominations vote and where their preferences lie on various issues. How grass-roots opinion reflects or differs from that of religious leaders is indicated in surveys of clergy and in analyses of the published statements of popular pastors and religious writers. Some attention has been paid to the kinds of issues religious lobbyists have pressed for at the federal level. Much attention has been given to the activities of pressure groups appealing to the public for support at various times, such as the Moral Majority and People for the American Way did in the 1980s. Congregational studies, while fairly sparse, have shed some light on the kinds of congregations most likely to engage in various political and community activities. A few efforts have also looked at the inner workings of church governing bodies. This work indicates the serious extent to which religion is involved in the public arena and the important role played by specific organizations in making this involvement possible. Because of practical considerations arising either from the need to address concrete issues or from the desire to be methodologically precise, much of this work has focused on very specific issues and organizations.

What is missing in this literature is the type of analysis that can only be made by taking a giant step backward from the specific issues and organizations that have been examined. Even from the perspective of one-step-removed, things always look different. It becomes possible to see that what we thought was a single yellow petal is part of a bouquet. We can also raise more speculative questions, like what if I yanked out this yellow flower and replaced it with a red one? We have to stand back to imagine what the result would be.

This is my aim. In this essay I want to raise some fundamental questions about public religion, asking what it is and where it comes from, and I want to reflect on these questions with as much naive curiosity as I can muster, given that I have spent most of my professional life as a student of religion and have been personally engaged in various religious organizations from the time I was a child. I call this an essay, even though as a whole it is longer than what we usually think of as an essay, because it is not a survey, a theory, or a study. A survey would try to present an overview, like a text book might, of the empirical literature currently in existence. In preparing this book I have read widely in this literature, but it did not seem to me that a sheer overview was the right thing to do, partly because there are already some fine textbooks that cover much of this literature and partly because I wanted to raise other questions that have seldom been addressed in the existing studies. A theory or theoretical treatise would try to develop a tightly interwoven set of logically dependent, empirically testable hypotheses about the subject under consideration. I cannot claim to have wanted to do that. My audience is neither social theorists nor some future generation of empiricists who would set out to test a body of preconceived generalizations. In some ways, of course, what I have done might be interpreted as a theory of public religion. But insofar as that is the case, it is more from having raised systematic questions than from having deduced answers from a body of theoretical literature. A study would of course have new data to present, but that is clearly not my aim either.

There is, however, a distinct perspective that I will be using as an orienting framework throughout the essay. The guiding assumption of this perspective is, as I have already hinted, that any of our cultural expressions, religious or otherwise, do not simply happen; they are produced. I will explain more fully in chapter 1 what exactly I mean by this, but let me say here that I will be drawing from the recent "production of culture" literature in sociology that emphasizes the role of organizations, professionals, power arrangements, and other social resources in generating cultural artifacts, such as music, books, and art. This perspective, I will argue, can also be applied usefully to the question of how organizations and communities shape the formation of public religion. I will not follow this literature rigidly, for I think the sacred differs in some important ways from these other kinds of culture. I do think, however, that we gain some significant insights by considering the sacred as something that is produced.

Varieties of Organizational Vehicles

The main assumptions of the cultural production approach are presented in chapter 1, and each of the following chapters takes up one of the major kinds of organizations that produce public religion. Although it is somewhat arbitrary to divide the religious world up in this fashion and we will need to consider in a concluding chapter how things all fit together, one of the important assumptions guiding this essay is that different kinds of religious organizations operate in different ways—need different resources from their host environments, set different goals, have different internal and external constraints, and accomplish some tasks more easily than others—and for this reason they make different contributions to the overall shape of public religion. My earlier example of "the Presbyterian church" will again serve to illustrate this point. Sometimes this phrase really means the denomination's general assembly or its Washington lobbying office; other times it stands as a kind of abbreviation for "local Presbyterian churches in the United States." How we think of the Presbyterian church's influence on public religion clearly depends on which of these we have in mind.

Chapters 2 through 6 deal respectively with the following kinds of organizations: congregations, hierarchies, special interests, academies, and public rituals. The last is generally not an organization in the same sense that a business firm, for example, is an organization, but it represents what sociologists would still consider a form of social organization in a broader sense — an organized or institutionalized set of activities — and thus provides a useful contrast with the kinds of organization dealt with in the chapters preceding it. These, it seems to me, represent the major social vehicles through which public religion is produced. Congregations are by far the most common and, insofar as they constitute the grass-roots basis of most other kinds of religious expression, may be the most consequential. *Hierarchies* is the term I am using to refer to those supracongregational entities that combine congregations into federations and provide coordination, communication, and governance. Denominational hierarchies, including committees, representative offices, deliberative bodies, and church judicial councils, are the clearest example, but interdenominational bodies often play these roles as well. Special interests must be considered a separate category because of the development in recent decades of a wide variety of parachurch groups, religious caucuses, professional organizations, and special purpose groups. Academies, by which I mean both religious and secular colleges and universities as well as seminaries and theological schools, must also be given special consideration because of the increasing importance of higher education as a source of religious expression.

Some obvious additions cry out for inclusion as well, but I will be dealing with most of these in conjunction with all of the five major kinds of organizations, rather than separately, because each is either a subunit within the others or a part of the environment that the others try to utilize in their efforts to shape public religion. For example, small groups are often the initial level of organization from which new religious ideas spring, and these are apparently becoming increasingly important in local congregations but may also be of growing significance in hierarchies or special interest organizations as well. They need to be considered, therefore, in each of the following chapters. Clergy will be treated in the same manner: although they play a very important role in producing public religion, their roles differ depending on the organizational context in which they occur. Other phenomena, such as the mass media and government agencies, are subsumed rather than treated separately for a different reason. Neither the media nor government agencies are primarily concerned with producing public religion. We cannot, for example, imagine them doing this in a society where there were no other religious institutions at all. (Even in communist societies where the government actively promulgated atheism, it did so against the backdrop of a very strong set of religious institutions.) Instead, both are important vehicles by which religious organizations produce, disseminate, or institutionalize particular aspects of public religion, and in this process both shape the eventual product as well. Indeed, religious organizations often try actively to influence the media and government as a way of achieving their larger goals. It therefore seems preferable to examine media and government in conjunction with each of the other forms of organization. It might also appear preferable, of course, to treat academies in the same manner. I have chosen to consider them separately, however, for two reasons: many colleges and universities (though a declining number), and of course theological schools and seminaries, are still officially chartered as religious entities and regard themselves as having some explicit role in the generation and dissemination of religious ideas; beyond this, a growing number of secular colleges and universities offer courses and degrees in religious studies, pay professors to do research on this topic, and feel it necessary to oversee in some way the religious life of their students. In so doing, they contribute significantly to the shaping of public religion.

What Is Public?

To speak of "public" religion or of the sacred in "public" life is to suggest the distinction between *public* and *private*. These are common terms, but they are used in a sufficient variety of ways that some clarity is needed before we can proceed to more specific issues. Insofar as *public* increasingly connotes social policy or the political, we need to distinguish these terms as well.

The most literal meaning of *public* is the people, as when we say that the American public consists of all its people. This is helpful in the present context because we will be considering religion and the sacred in their collective manifestations and influences, that is, the religious expressions that are held widely among people and pertain to their collective identity as a people. It is not necessary that these expressions include all the people (say, atheists and wiccans as well as Catholics and Protestants) anymore than it is necessary for the public to include everyone living in a society at a given time. Generally, the public is some significant gathering of people or some segment of the population that has a distinct identity. For purposes of voting we might consider the public to be people of voting age, whereas the public implicit in the thinking of the National Football League might include a somewhat broader range of ages. What *public* means is itself a matter of cultural definition. In what sense it actually differs from the individuals of which it is composed is also a matter of definition. The public can be a collective entity that actually has little sense of itself as anything but an aggregation of separate individuals. Critics of the term *public opinion*, for example, point out that it is an oxymoron because the opinions expressed are generally held by separate individuals and never given voice except to a pollster. This criticism also hints at a second meaning of the term.

Public also connotes openness or accessibility. Public land belongs to the people; public space is a place where people are free to assemble; public facilities are open to the public; to put on a public face means adopting an expression you are willing for others to see; newspapers disclose information by uncovering a story and printing it so that everyone has access to it. Again, the point is not that everyone living in a whole society actually has access; the access can be potential, or it can mean simply that a private individual is unable to guard it completely. This is what we mean when we say a company's stock is traded publicly. Anyone with the required funds can purchase a share, rather than its being owned entirely by one family. In religious contexts to say that something is public also means that it is out in the open, rather than being buried in the subjective consciousness of the individual.

These two meanings of *public* go together. If something pertains to the people or to a collectivity, it is more likely to be open and accessible as well. The exceptions are "official secrets," and these are despised because they are relevant to our concerns and yet not open to us. By the same token, if something is made open and accessible, then it also in a sense becomes the property of a collectivity and in this way is capable of influencing the collectivity. Someone in a support group, for example, may share a very personal emotion or experience; once it is out in the open, it is no longer that person's alone. It belongs to the group, and so the group may define norms of nondisclosure or anonymity to prevent it from spreading to a wider public.

This example also points to the fact that public and private can never be entirely separated. *American* is surely an adjective that is used commonly with reference to such nouns as *public* or *people*, yet I am individually an American too, and some of what this means is, as it were, inside of me. Social scientists would say a public identity, or aspects of the collectivity in which one resides, can be internalized, becoming part of one's personal self-concept as well. Conversely, people who shared something intimate from their private experiences are externalizing that event, turning it into the shared history of the collectivity. In focusing on public religion, therefore, we will not be able to ignore private religion entirely.

If the public and the private are always connected, it is nevertheless important to recognize that they are probably more distinct, and problematic, in modern settings than in most of the societies preceding ours historically. This is because the anonymity of modern society allows us to keep things more fully to ourselves than would have been possible in most earlier settings. Indeed, one sees a dramatic increase in discussions of the private and its relation to the public just at that point (in the eighteenth century in most western European societies) when the city was beginning to make life more anonymous. There is, for example, a huge disparity between Rousseau's private and public life that is impossible to conceive of in the life of Augustine, Aquinas, Luther, or Calvin. We still live in this post-Enlightenment world, where our inner thoughts need never be expressed in public and where we can even play roles in public life that have little to do with how we think and feel in the deepest recesses of our inner lives. We have also been influenced by the Romantics, who taught us that the inner life is also especially valuable and unique. Our individuality is not just a reflection of being, say, American but something that wells up from within and distinguishes us fundamentally from every other person who may also go by this label.

It is for this reason that many observers of modern society (our own and others) think the relationship between public and private has become problematic. With so much emphasis on our individuality, and with so much of what individuality means being located in the inner or subjective consciousness, it becomes easier for people to retreat from public life or to engage in it with little affect or serious involvement. Intimate family relations, sex, or a good mystery novel become much more interesting to us than the cause of world peace or the debt crisis in Latin America. The same is true in matters of the sacred. People meditate, pray, arrive at their own unique beliefs about God, and even make up religions they name after themselves, but are they nearly as interested in religious institutions or God's purposes for our nation?

As it happens, there is also a third (and almost wholly neglected) meaning of *public* that goes to the heart of these concerns about the separation of private and public life. In its Latin derivation, *public* is associated with the idea of having been altered, probably in the way that an adult is altered by having gone through puberty. Hence, the term *public* also connotes the kind of adult responsibility that we do not normally expect of children. This is why we associate being a public official with taking responsibility for the interests of a body of people, or why playing a public role conjures up images of responsibility to, and for, some group. To escape into one's private world is an escape because it removes one temporarily from this kind of responsibility. To speak of public religion, in contrast, is to suggest that individuals need to take responsibility for the good of their society instead of escaping into private spirituality and that the public arena itself must reinforce this sense of responsibility among individuals and to whatever is sacred and transcendent about their collective values.

Several of the terms already mentioned, such as *private companies* or *public officials*, suggest the need also to consider how meanings of *public* overlap with such terms as *politics* or *public policy*. *Politics* generally refers to governmental organizations and their functions, including those that may exist at federal, state, county, and municipal levels, as well as political parties. These organizations subsume the usual executive, legislative, and judicial functions that make up the three branches of U.S. government, yet they are generally considered by social scientists to include something cultural as well, that which is often described as ultimate societal authority or the legitimate use of coercion. A tendency to equate *public* with *political* derives from two sources. Historically, the two were virtually synonymous in Hegelian conceptions of civil society, in which civil society was

centrally coordinated by government agencies (such as those prominent in Prussian society) but also encompassed every other part of
society except for private economic entities and the family. In this
conception, it might be noted, religion was inseparable from state
and civil society, making any notion of public religion redundant.
In such societies as Germany and Sweden, it might also be noted,
civil society and the *state* are still terms that can be used interchangeably. The more contemporary source of overlap between *public* and
political is the fact that government has expanded in recent decades
to subsume more and more of civil society. In virtually all industrial democracies government revenues and expenditures make up a
much larger share of personal income and Gross National Product,
respectively, than they did a half-century ago, an increasing array of
services is provided by government (from military defense and police
protection to highway building, regulation of public airways, environmental protection, prevention of discrimination, and services
for the indigent and elderly), more and more of the labor force is
employed by government agencies, science and education are vig-
orously promoted by government, and citizens look increasingly to
the courts to settle their grievances.

When people speak of public religion or of the sacred in the public
arena nowadays, they often have in mind some connection between
religion and politics. This is simply because politics has become so
influential in determining the course of public affairs that attempting
to shape governmental decisions seems like the best way of making
religion's voice heard. It would be more precise to say that religion is
attempting to influence public policy—that is, specific bills or court
cases or executive initiatives regarded as ways of implementing collective values—and that politics is the means by which such efforts
are made. Policy is the end, while politics is the means. Religious
bodies, therefore, may not be interested in gaining political power
for its own sake, but they engage in lobbying or voter registration or
petition drives as a way of securing passage of a favored law deemed
to be in the interest of peace, justice, morality, or some other religious value.

Discussions of religion and politics have become more important than ever before in American history because an entire industry of lobbyists, lawyers, church bureaucrats, and academics has
emerged to speak for and against religious interests on matters of

public policy. To frame the issue of public religion entirely in these terms is to be overly narrow, however. Neither *politics* nor *public policy* means exactly the same thing as *public*. Equating these terms therefore causes one to lose sight of other ways in which religion may be present in the public arena.

Instead of the civil society image that equates politics and the public, a better way of understanding the distinctive characteristics of religion in American society is to think in terms of three primary sectors: state, market, and voluntary sectors. The state can be understood in much the same way we have already considered it, encompassing politics and the policy ends to which politics is directed; the market, or economic realm, is, in American society at least, sharply distinguished from the state (although the two often work together) by virtue of its profit orientation, its system of pricing based on supply and demand, and the legal restrictions that prevent its use of ultimate coercive power. The voluntary sector is a separate realm, including the nation's religious organizations that are constitutionally demarcated from the state and legally distinguished from the profit realm, plus vast numbers of formal nonprofit organizations and informal charities, associations, and communities. In this conception all three sectors may contribute to the public arena, and all three involve activities that are more clearly considered the private, or personal domain, of individuals and families. For example, political, economic, and voluntary organizations can be concerned with improving the quality of mattresses on which people sleep—a private function—or they can be concerned with initiating or limiting new weapons systems said to protect the whole society from foreign conquest—a public function. The public arena therefore consists primarily of the process of discussing collective values, that is, those that pertain to the whole society or to some substantial segment of society and are open and accessible by virtue of being discussed.

An important implication of considering the public arena in this fashion is that several new sources of potential tension involving religion are highlighted. In addition to the tension between private, subjectivized religiosity and the public expression of religion to which we have already alluded, there are tensions between the voluntary sector and the state, between the voluntary sector and the marketplace, and between religion and other organizations operating in the voluntary sector. These tensions arise because all the various sec-

tors and organizations are to some extent concerned with influencing public discourse about collective values. The state or political
sphere is thus not simply a means that religious entities use to pursue policy ends; it is an actor in its own right, with interests and
objectives that may well differ from those of religious organizations.
Accordingly, religious organizations may find themselves struggling
not only with other pressure groups but with vested political interests as well. The state-religion boundary is not, however, the only
zone along which conflict may arise. Tensions with the economic
sphere may be equally important, especially as norms of profitability,
consumption, material success, or even efficiency move from the
marketplace into the religious realm. In addition, religious organizations may increasingly find themselves in competition with other
voluntary associations also trying to provide social services, promote community, or make their values known to the public at large.
In this competition religious organizations are unlikely to function
as monoliths but instead engage in the public arena in a variety of
ways, some political and some nonpolitical.

Why the Public Is Precarious

Seeing Congress debate legislative bills or reading the Supreme
Court's latest rulings, we may find it hard to believe that anything
could be wrong with the public arena in which such debates and
rulings take place. Democratic societies provide broad settings in
which collective values can be discussed, and the more affluent of
these societies give people the wherewithal to understand public debate, to participate in it, and to enjoy its fruits. Yet social observers
express concern about the vitality of the public sphere, not simply
because it gives them something to do but also because the public is
an exceedingly precarious institution.

One of the most serious sources of concern in recent decades,
as already noted, is the tendency for people in modern democratic
societies to retreat from the public arena into their own private
lives. Like most behavior, this tendency is rooted in both "pull" and
"push" factors. The pull factors that draw people into their private
realms include the widespread emphasis on consumerism, which encourages people to work harder to make higher incomes to pay for

the labor-saving devices that allow them to work harder; the attractions of romantic and familial intimacy in a world where self esteem is increasingly dependent on intermittent interpersonal reinforcement; and the expressive individualism that encourages individuals to spend more time cultivating their inner selves. The push factors that drive people away from engagement in public life include massive increases in the scale of government and corporate organizations, leading the average individual to believe there is little possibility of making any difference in the public arena, and the growing tendency for social policies to be determined with some effectiveness by professional and technical bureaucrats rather than in genuinely open public debate. The joint pressure of all these factors is to encourage individuals to remove themselves from public life, thereby leaving it in the hands of a relatively small group that may well not represent the public at large.

The dangers attendant upon this tendency toward privatization are aggravated by other pressures that bear directly on the nature of public discourse itself. The enormous growth in central government activity that has taken place over the past half-century has come about (to a degree) because of sincere interest on the part of many for the welfare of society, but this same growth has subjected increasing areas of social life to the norms of political expedience and bureaucratic concerns with efficiency. These, to be sure, are among the high values of modern societies, but they are only a small and unrepresentative portion of these values. What may be cost-effective in the short run may not be beneficial to the whole society in the long run. Time and again examples of such shortsightedness in the political sector are evident in the news media. Moreover, relying on bureaucratic agencies to determine basic societal goals and policies makes these goals and policies subject to the internal limitations of such agencies. The stalemate in the United States between the legislative and executive branches during the 1980s is but one example. On the economic side, free market forces are also poorly designed to ensure the vitality of public discourse about basic collective values. Although business leaders often voice the view that a healthy society is in their interest as well, considerations of who will pay the cost and how these costs will redound against the position of firms in competitive world markets usually take precedence in practice. Indeed, it is instructive that the United States has generally been attracted to Japan, a society in

which the public sphere has been constricted to the point that virtually nothing other than economic growth can be discussed, far more
than to societies like Sweden, Great Britain, or France, where government places more serious checks on the economic sector.

If, as Alexis de Tocqueville suggested more than 150 years ago,
voluntary associations and active participation in community organizations are the key to a healthy democratic public sphere, then the
growth of bureaucratic government and the simultaneous spread of
the profit sector should be cause for serious concern. The growth in
these sectors would suggest a correlative shrinkage of the voluntary
sector. Yet the conclusion that has emerged from numerous studies
of this sector is that it is not so much declining—in fact it has often
shown budgetary and organizational growth—as it is changing in
character. With an increasing share of funding for nonprofit organizations coming from government, often amounting to at least half
of all such funding, and with profit firms engaged in competition
to provide social services, the voluntary sector appears to be subject
to most of the same government regulations and cost considerations
that organizations in the other two sectors are. One cannot help
wondering, therefore, whether the voluntary sector can contribute
any more freely, openly, or creatively to the expression of public
values than government or business can.

The Role of Religion

Religious organizations are perhaps subject to the same pressures
that appear to be undermining the vitality of the public sphere more
generally: private spirituality and devotional piety often seem to be
more vital than participation in the public work of religious institutions; government increasingly tells religious organizations what
they can and cannot do; and these same organizations seem compelled to worry more and more about competition with one another
and with turning in favorable balance sheets at the end of each fiscal
year. Yet religion is uniquely suited to retain a distinctive role in the
public sphere.

Constitutional separation of church and state ensures some degree
of autonomy, while legal restrictions (largely from tax-exemption

laws) prevent religious organizations from engaging directly in for-profit economic activities. Religion is thus a somewhat protected zone in which issues can be debated in ways that may be critical of established government policies or may simply defy the logic of bureaucratic norms in either the political or economic sectors. On occasion religious leaders have been able to mobilize vast reform efforts from this protected zone, as they did during the civil rights movement or the protest movement against the Vietnam War. Efforts to provide sanctuary to refugees from strife-ridden countries or to cultivate greater respect for the disadvantaged or people with alternative life-styles serve as additional examples. Equally important, religious organizations can espouse deep human values, such as love, mercy, and forgiveness, that are seldom evident at all in government and business circles.

Apart from the opportunities that may exist for religious organizations to influence collective values, an even more compelling case can be made for the importance of the sacred to the vitality of any society. Historically, two contributions in particular have frequently been identified: a strong sense of the sacred has been the basis for an autonomous public sphere itself, and this sense of the sacred has also served a vital prophetic function. The importance of the former is attested by the fact that public space developed in Western societies chiefly because free religious organizations demanded that limits be placed on the state to ensure freedom of conscience. The prophetic function has been exercised repeatedly, with religious leaders taking up causes as diverse as the criminalization of dueling to the advocacy of gender equality, always pointing to a higher law and a more transcendent conception of justice than that embodied in the current laws of the land.

Were the sacred to disappear from the public realm, both the public realm itself and its sense of justice would be greatly diminished. It is thus for both social and spiritual reasons that we need to consider the ways in which religious communities and organizations participate in public life: the social reasons derive from our sense that a healthy society depends on this participation; the spiritual reasons, from the conviction, widely held by many in our society, that the sacred itself is an intrinsic value.

Central Issues

Each of the five forms of religious organization—congregations, hierarchies, special interests, academies, and public rituals—to be considered in the following chapters participate in the public arena, attempting to make the sacred manifest in public life, from a distinctive niche in the social environment. We do not have to engage in functionalist reasoning to suggest that these forms have become differentiated from one another because each fulfills functions somewhat different from the others'; we can see without any special insight at all that congregations and academies, for example, play different roles. It is for this reason that the particular contributions of these organizational types, and the challenges facing them, deserve special attention, instead of merely speaking of religion as a uniform entity. There are, however, a several common issues that we will want to consider for all five of these organizational types.

We will begin by paying explicit attention to the fact that none of these five organizational types is itself monolithic. Each is characterized by internal diversity: congregations come in all sizes, hale from different theological traditions, employ varying governing and decision-making styles, and utilize their leaders and members in different ways. When we speak of religious pluralism, we mean internal diversity as much as diversity in denominations, faiths, and beliefs. Our intention is not to survey all the specific variations in American religion (were that possible) but to suggest the main dimensions of variation as background for considering the multiplicity of ways in which religious organizations might contribute to the public sphere.

We will then consider a cluster of questions arising from the fact that religious organizations—like all organizations—operate in an institutional environment, attempting to implement various activities and programs by extracting resources from their environments (members, communities, constituencies), and in the process they seek to address certain audiences or publics more than others. These questions take us to the heart of *how* public religion is produced. It is here in the trenches, so to speak, that the hard decisions are made, but this is also where the role of the social becomes most important. Too often in the past, this influence has been conceived of in connection with the individual believer, whose beliefs and experiences are shaped by class background, regional subcultures, or ethnic heritage. Our attention here will be drawn to the ways in which social conditions influence *organizations*, which, in turn, may shape individuals' beliefs or may try to play a direct role in public life.

The chief question we then want to examine in each chapter is what sort of contribution these religious organizations make. What expressions of the sacred do they bring into the public sphere? And how do their organizational characteristics and their location in the society enhance, delimit, or shape the nature of these expressions? Some of these manifestations will be intended, others will be by-products of the activities in which religious organizations are engaged. We will want to consider both, again taking a broad view of what the sacred is, whether it takes a specifically religious form or not.

Finally, we will consider the contribution of each organizational form to public religion in a more temporal context, asking what the main challenges are that arise from an increasingly complex, and perhaps secular, society. This question will force us to focus on the ways in which religious organizations may adapt to the wider society. Since religious organizations are never just reactive but are also dynamic, creative entities in themselves, we must also consider their prospects for innovation.

1

Cultural Production

Social scientists interested in cultural issues have come increasingly to adopt what is called a "production of culture" approach to their topic. The central claim of this perspective is that culture does not simply happen or merely exist but is the outcome of deliberate human activity. Studies approaching culture in this way often disagree with one another about the particular factors that shape culture, but the perspective itself is undoubtedly the most widely shared of all approaches to the subject. To understand why this perspective has come to be regarded so highly and how it may contribute to a better understanding of public religion, we need to begin with a brief look at the ways in which culture and religion have generally been conceived in the social science literature.

A Glimpse at the Past

The earliest social scientists were certainly aware that ideas and beliefs come about because of human action; indeed, one of the leading premises on which the social sciences was founded was the claim that society is the source of ideas instead of ideas having an independent existence of some kind. Reflecting the philosophical skepticism of their day, social scientists of the nineteenth century were often particularly keen on demonstrating the dependence of religious beliefs on social factors. Karl Marx made assertions about the ways in which religious leaders shaped the character of modern religious belief and how they were in turn products of the economic circumstances in which these leaders lived. Max Weber was fundamentally more interested in the effects of various ethical systems on the shape of human society than in the social origins of these systems, but he also wrote imaginatively of how the social role of the prophet differed from that of the priest, how the two generated different styles of religious thought, the ways in which such rising social classes as artisans or warriors became the carriers of new ethical orientations, and the influence that bureaucracies could have on belief systems in modern societies. His contemporary Émile Durkheim wrote perceptively about the ways in which experiences of social authority reinforced certain conceptions of the sacred, the importance of the church or some comparable body of believers, and the role of ritual activity in sustaining distinctions between the sacred and the profane.

The American social scientists and students of religion who contributed the first major studies of faith in the United States were generally inspired by practical considerations, but they were also led to emphasize the same social factors that their European predecessors had identified. H. Richard Niebuhr adroitly demonstrated how American social divisions, particularly along class, regional, and racial lines, reinforced the presence of distinct denominational orientations in religion. H. Paul Douglass, though less concerned with religious ideas themselves, pioneered significant work on the relations between local churches and their host environments, often anticipating what has in more recent years been recognized as an ecological approach to organizations. Others in the same period showed how urbanization was altering the character of American religion and did community studies linking common religious orientations to particular churches, holidays and festivals, education levels, and occupations. There was at this point a strong basis on which to build the more recent cultural production perspective. Indeed, it probably would have seemed unnecessary in this period to argue that beliefs were socially produced because that was the underlying premise of the new social scientific approaches. Yet this premise was altered and almost nearly eclipsed by developments that took place during the middle decades of the twentieth century.

Three of these developments are especially worthy of note. First, there was a strong tendency among the more theoretically minded social scientists to reconceptualize culture as a kind of broad, all-encompassing system of norms and values. In this view, culture was not so much anything specific that anyone had produced as it was a set of preexisting assumptions, widely shared and long enduring, that provided tacit explanations for why societies prospered or failed and that guided behavior into various channels. Second, especially among students of religion, new perspectives rooted in phenomenology and hermeneutics stressed the importance of looking internally at the composition of symbol systems to understand their meanings better. Third, also among students of religion, new methods of conducting surveys and public opinion polls opened possibilities for examining the content of individuals' religious beliefs and attitudes, and to the extent that social factors were still assumed to influence these opinions, they were primarily operationalized as matters of individual socialization, such as family background and schooling. The upshot of these developments was to deemphasize the role of communities and organizations and to conceive of religious beliefs either as autonomous systems or as the result only of broad, implicit, unconscious, and indirect social influences.

The rediscovery, as it were, of cultural artifacts explicitly produced in social contexts came in the 1970s, not by students of religion but by social scientists studying music, art, museums, and the like, where the evidence that culture was in fact produced was simply too compelling to ignore. Indeed, the entrenchment of established notions of culture was evidenced by the fact that the production perspective came primarily from social scientists interested in complex organizations and social movements who paid more attention to the structure of these organizations than to the actual artifacts being produced, and this work was for a considerable time strongly resisted by those who claimed to be authorities on culture itself. Among students of religion it was primarily the wave of new religious movements in the late 1960s and 1970s that led to new questions being asked about the resources on which belief systems may depend. For this reason the role of communities and organizations has continued to be stressed more by students of religious movements than in studies of dominant or established religious systems. Only in recent years has the decline in some of these bodies begun to generate interest in such questions, and even then work has often continued to focus on beliefs and attitudes, as if these were the determinants of denominational strength rather than the converse. Questions about the role of religious bodies in the political sphere have also begun to

redirect some attention to organizational resources, but as yet these
questions have also been treated mainly in terms of political opinions, issues, and attitudes instead of generating studies of communities and organizations. The cultural production perspective has thus
progressed far more in studies of other kinds of culture, such as art,
literature, and political ideology, than in applications to the understanding of religion.

The Production of Culture

The best way to understand the distinctive contribution of the cultural production school is by considering the space it opens up between private and public expressions of culture. In classical understandings of culture it has always been recognized that culture exists,
as it were, both inside us and outside us at the same time. When we
think up an idea, say, a solution to the math problem presented to us
in our homework, that idea exists inside us; it is part of our subjective
being, our thoughts, the unspoken ruminations of our mind. The
same is true of our beliefs about God or the prayers we say quietly
to ourselves: perhaps we sense God's loving presence, so that part of
our subjective experience is a feeling of warmth and well-being; perhaps we develop an image in our heads of what this being is like, and
that helps concretize our thought processes, making it possible to
communicate internally with this being. We would, in this sense, say
also that our concept of God is internalized, a part of our own being
or sense of self or personal identity. The external or public part of
these beliefs, the ones that exist outside us, consist of any utterances
or gestures we might make to communicate these inner experiences
to someone else and any objects or events in the surrounding world
that we internalize into our own thinking. I have an image in my
head of the math problem in my book, but the fact that it exists there
in the book for anyone who might be interested in seeing it means
that it is public (or objective) as well as private and subjective. When
I tell others about my belief in God, I externalize that belief, and
when I pray out loud, I do the same. Someone else could repeat my
statements or my prayers, even write them down, record them, or
publish them, so their existence might outlast mine. The image in
my head, moreover, is likely to be only partly mine, unless I am su-

premely isolated and creative. Most of us form the pictures in our heads by seeing pictures in books or on television or having them painted for us by writers and poets. These are all facets of culture that someone else has externalized, making them publicly available.

The cultural production approach takes this separation of the private and the public one step further. To speak, for example, of artists' externalizing an image in their heads so that it is an objective cultural artifact leaps very quickly—too quickly—from the internal to the external, from the subjective to the objective. The transition happens conceptually in a single instant, whereas in reality it may take much longer, or even if it is instantaneous, the film projector needs to be stopped and then moved forward one frame at a time to see more precisely what has transpired. What *has* transpired? How was it possible for a particular person to be an artist in the first place? What training was involved? What financial backing made it possible to obtain this training? Who provided the physical space in which the painting was accomplished? What materials and technologies were used? Who commissioned the painting? How did the commissioning agent find out about this artist? In what ways were all these social transactions a factor in the content of the painting itself? These are the questions with which cultural production studies are concerned.

In the case of an artist who deliberately sets out to produce a cultural product the considerations raised by this perspective are relatively straightforward. Since the act of producing art, like that of producing anything, is a kind of work, involving an expenditure of energy, the initial questions that must be addressed concern resources required to engage in this work. Most of these resources radiate out in concentric circles from the immediate act of production itself. One can thus ask about tools and materials used directly to create the product or, at a step removed, the training and the financial backing needed to learn how to use these tools and materials. Social scientists, unlike artists themselves, are especially interested in the person using the materials, perhaps more than in understanding whether a certain kind of acrylics or oils was used. The person, or actor, becomes a focal point around which many other social influences converge. For example, artists are among other things people who have come to think of themselves as artists, to internalize a particular social role; hence, questions arise about the nature of that role, the mentors that transmitted it, and the models it conveyed. At somewhat greater distance from the production process itself, social scientists are also interested in how societal configurations affected the availability of the resources that went into the process. Instead of asking how a particular person came to be trained as an artist, the observer would want to know whether an increase in affluence levels in the society had made it possible for more talented individuals to seek such training in the first place or perhaps whether some group had lobbied the government to provide grants to aspiring artists.

It should be evident that many of these questions arise when the cultural artifact being produced is not art but religion. When a preacher delivers a sermon on Sunday morning to a packed audience of suburban parishioners, the questions about resources are much the same as those pertaining to an artist. Who provided the training? What pays the preacher's salary? How did the auditorium get built? Who pays the mortgage and the utility bills? Does the economy encourage talented individuals to seek training as clergy? Did some group lobby the municipal government to ensure that zoning laws would not prevent people from parking around the church on Sunday morning?

In another sense, though, religion may seem quite different from artists' producing paintings. The art world places a premium on creativity, so artists are encouraged and rewarded to be inventive. Their inventions do not simply happen spontaneously; they are the result of deliberate effort. How can this be compared with walking along a country road some starlit night and suddenly experiencing the presence of the sacred? Or, even in the case of a preacher, how does it square with the idea that the preacher does not invent God but allows God to speak, the sermon becoming therefore much more an *enactment* of the sacred than a production?

On the surface these examples point to deep differences between religion and art, yet closer examination indicates that the same questions might be asked about certain kinds of art, thus suggesting the value of complicating the straightforward view of cultural production that we have just been considering. The person experiencing God on a country road is like an artist who has a sudden flash of inspiration; artists and mystics alike refer to such numinous experiences as moments of awe and mystery when a force outside their own conscious striving seems to take over. The point is not that the artist or the mystic engaged in no deliberate effort. They were consciously striving for something, just not for the outcome that happened. Volumes have of course been written about these experiences and the conditions under which they occur; the important issue for our purposes is simply that cultural production results in both products and by-products, that is, intended results and unintended results. This will be a significant consideration when we turn to the organizations that produce public religion in our society. Some of what they produce is deliberate, and some is unplanned and unexpected. In both cases resources are expended, and social circumstances influence what happens. We can ask about the resources making it possible for someone to take a walk on a starlit night and to be favorably disposed to interpreting something as the divine presence just as well as we can ask about the wherewithal needed to preach a sermon.

Preachers who allow God to speak through them and whose sermons, clerical garb, and liturgical style do more to *enact* the sacred than to produce it raise an equally important consideration. It is difficult for us to imagine someone in a different cultural milieu—Moses, for example—"enacting" the sacred. God spoke to Moses from the burning bush and gave the Ten Commandments on tablets of stone. According to the tradition Moses did not feel a vague stirring within himself and then act out the voice of God. (Perhaps that is exactly what happened, but it is not the way tradition tells it.) In modern culture, however, the sacred is less visible and less audible; we also place more stock in the inner voices or sentiments that seem to embody the divine within ourselves. The sacred consequently often does appear to be an emanation or an externalization of something from within. It is so much ours that we have to act it out, perhaps behaviorally and emotionally as well as verbally. Yet this too is not altogether unlike our conception of modern art. In an earlier era artists tried to represent something on canvas that was presumed to exist in the external world. The more recent contrast between realist art and expressivist art has, however, been evoked by the blurring of this internal-external distinction, so that more of the creative insight is presumed to come from within, and artists thus express (or enact) that insight instead of merely representing something external. This too is an important modification for conventional conceptions of cultural production, but it does not negate the value of the production perspective. It merely indicates that in considering religion, we need to be especially mindful of the ways in which communities and organizations may expressively enact the sacred.

Thus far I have drawn attention only to the producers of culture and the resources on which they depend, but the cultural production approach also stresses the importance of readers, consumers, and other audiences. Their influence is likely to be twofold: as patrons and purchasers of cultural products, they supply tangible resources to producers; as audiences with certain tastes, perspectives, or dispositions, they may influence what the artist or writer produces because that person anticipates what will be pleasing to them. In thinking about public religion, we should consider who the relevant audiences or publics may be. In one instance it may be the assembled audience at a worship service; in another it may be preachers' internalized conception of the broader American public (which they may hope to influence or which may hear about their remarks from their parishioners). How consumers and producers are linked is also a critical issue. Indeed, in social histories of art and literature one of the most decisive factors identified in theories of cultural change has been the shift in consumer relations away from patron-client patterns toward a market-oriented system. Religious culture remains very much in the patron-client mode insofar as time and money are still provided on a voluntary basis, but fee-for-service relations are also becoming more common.

It is also important to recognize that cultural production is a *process* and that different influences may become relevant at different points in this process. Were the issue simply the production of a single painting or book, we might be content to telescope this process into a single or short-term transaction, but the issue is often not about one product but about a whole genre of literature or an evolving pattern in music composition. Under these circumstances observers have had to consider the factors that might have led to innovation in the first place, how a variety of innovations competed with one another, what forces resulted in some of these innovations being favored more than others, and eventually how something innovative became the established, conventional, or predominant form. Organizations concerned with producing the sacred are inevitably constrained on a day-to-day basis to focus on tonight's business meeting, tomorrow's phone calls to Capitol Hill, and next Sunday's sermon. But these are all limited skirmishes in the larger war in which religious organizations are engaged to sustain the sacred in an otherwise secular environment. The cultural production approach draws attention to the various phases of this overall process.

The process nature of cultural production means that influences and restrictions on the production of public religion may enter in different ways at different points. For example, in earlier times the state often tried to prevent preachers from producing verbal products (sermons) in the first place; later, when instruments of mass terror became more effective, states tried to prevent people from becoming the consumers of these products. In many totalitarian societies clergy have often been left alone, but people were punished if they came to listen, losing their government jobs, public education, and the like. In democratic societies neither the producers nor the consumers of public religion are controlled in these ways, but government may regulate the dissemination process or allow the media to influence this process. Religious organizations have done fairly well at retaining control over the verbal transmission of their own messages, but the media often intervene and supply alternative interpretations of public statements or actions. When a denominational policy statement is generated as a teaching tool to be used within the church, for example, the media might take it and subject it to a different kind of scrutiny, commentary, and criticism.

Organizations, Environments, and Competition

In giving an overview of the cultural production approach, I have illustrated it in simplest form by taking examples of individual artists, writers, or preachers engaged in generating certain texts and symbols. These individuals do indeed play an exceptionally significant role; without them it is hard to imagine committees, agencies, or bureaucratic offices doing much to improve the cultural life of the nation. Yet it is chiefly to organizations that we must look to understand how public religion, or any other cultural form, is produced. This is because individual producers generally require organizations to secure and orchestrate the resources they need, and organizations in turn generate other organizations because of the competition that is inherent in securing resources from an environment in which the most valued resources are always in short supply. I alluded briefly to this competition in the introduction; let us consider it here with greater precision.

Although it is always possible to focus on specific persons, or even specific organizations, and see them in competition with other individuals and organizations, the starting point that gives us the greatest purchase on this aspect of social life is to conceive of a whole field or industry of competing organizations, for example, all the religious congregations in a given city or denomination rather than any particular congregation. Doing this sensitizes us immediately to the importance of their environment. The environment can sustain only so many of these organizations; *how many* depends on the resources available in that environment. The simultaneous existence of these organizations also sensitizes us to three kinds of interactions or processes that are likely to develop: selective adaptation, isomorphism, and specialization.

Selective adaptation is the process whereby organizations in competition with one another succeed in extracting resources from their host environment, with the result that over time some organizations cease to exist, while others take over a disproportionate share of the available resources. It is this process that results in some level of "fit" between the ideas that an organization produces and the environment in which it produces those ideas. In this view people do not simply adapt their ideas to their social circumstances because of peer pressure or because they want to fit in; their ideas adapt gradually, and often blindly, because some organizations are better able to secure resources than others are. Two of the most prominent examples in American religious history were nineteenth-century Baptists and Methodists who adapted to the individualistic and heterogeneous environments of the expanding American frontier much more successfully than did those in the more established and class-based denominations, such as the Episcopal church. Selective adaptation also suggests the presence of a kind of market mechanism operating even among such nonmarket organizations as churches. This is not because churches in some way sell their products in a competitive pricing situation but because they do compete with one another for the time and money of a limited number of parishioners who may be willing to give such time and money. This competition is often good for the state of religion as a whole; it means, for example, that religious organizations are likely to try to do well in their host environments. But it also means that some organizations that might have a particularly "true" or "powerful" conception of the sacred will nevertheless fail to survive against the competition of other organizations that simply fit in better with their cultural surroundings. The scope of competition is also likely to pit religious organizations against secular ones that may also be better suited to survival in a secular culture.

Isomorphism is the process, also associated with organizational competition, by which these organizations come to resemble one another in form or substance. Although this process is always balanced by specialization (which we will consider momentarily), it is perhaps paradoxically one of the ways in which organizations elevate their chances of survival in a competitive situation. The paradox lies in the fact that organizations might be expected to differentiate themselves from one another (and they do) by, for example, trying to produce a more attractive or distinctive product; yet one way to ensure at least a minimal share of the resources available in any environment is to make one's organization indistinguishable from all the others. Among the manufacturers of breakfast cereals, for example, nearly all the major companies package their products in rectangular boxes of about the same size and weight, agree to place these products on the same shelf at the supermarket, and stay largely within the same range as far as the nutritional content of their products is concerned. Among American churches nearly all hold their services on the same day of the week at approximately the same hour and include preaching and singing in those services. The function of isomorphism is twofold: it helps identify an organization as part of a certain set or system (for example, as a church, a school, or a basketball team); second, it generally signals conformity with some larger norms in the institutional environment of these organizations. Cereal packages contain lists of ingredients because of laws requiring them to do so; churches may contain ramps for the handicapped for similar reasons. Conformity is also generated by norms expressing values and practices known to be important in the society. For example, most churches could probably do with less elaborate buildings (or with no buildings at all), but the presence of an architecturally splendid edifice in an affluent neighborhood signals to outsiders that one can be materially successful and a good church member at the same time.

Specialization is the countertendency to isomorphism. It is the process, again under competitive conditions, by which organizations acquire a distinctive niche in the environment by performing a special role in some larger division of labor. One cereal maker may try to carve out a niche in the health food or dietetic market, while another strives to capture the children's market. Similarly, the church on one corner may be better known for its music program, while the church across the street may specialize in youth ministries. Specialization, as these examples suggest, is more likely to develop in heterogeneous social environments. Were there no youth in the community, the second church might also have to become better in offering music. Specialization can be a source of cooperation as well, for it minimizes competition to some extent, but it also leaves any particular organization somewhat dependent on others to fulfill different tasks and, indeed, to supply it with some of the resources it cannot generate by itself. Lacking enough young voices, the one church may have to recruit youth from the other, for example.

In combination these three processes—selective adaptation, isomorphism, and specialization—help us see that the products generated by any particular organization are not merely the result of random efforts by talented leaders or exceptionally clever committees; these products are part of a larger system, and which ones find the light of day depends very much on whether their organizations are successful in coping with the exigencies of their social environments. We have already seen that the richness or leanness of an environment in terms of extractable resources can be crucial to the survival of organizations. It is also the case that some organizations may develop strategies to cope more effectively with lean times, while other organizations do better living off the fat of the land. Heterogeneity is itself terribly important, and new populations or issues that add to this diversity are always likely to encourage new organizations to appear to fill those niches.

All this also suggests that the environment in which any culture-producing organization exists is likely to be highly uncertain or at best unstable. As any church administrator knows, churches can suddenly become obsolete because people move out of the neighborhoods in which they are located and refuse to travel long distances to continue attending them. Or religious agencies that drew talented personnel and generous donations because they were in the forefront of advocacy on a particular position suddenly become pariahs as political winds shift in unfavorable directions. This is one reason why organizations exist in the first place. They are somewhat better suited to surviving uncertain times than individuals are. The lone pastor standing on the street corner may move on when the neighborhood changes, but the presence of a church building on that corner means that there is still a place for people to worship and that if one group leaves, another may move in. Or if the neighborhood remains the same, that lone pastor may suffer a heart attack some night, causing the ministry to end, whereas the pastor heading an established organization will simply be replaced. Uncertainty, as well as heterogeneity, also causes organizations to develop structures capable of transcending specific issues or occupying delimited niches. The federated structures known as denominations allow a particular kind of religious message to be carried on in a new part of the country even when the population in another area declines. At the local level churches often try not to specialize too narrowly, becoming isomorphic with one another instead but doing so in a way that includes a variety of functions broad enough that the larger organization will not die when one of these functions ceases to be appealing.

If these processes sound too mechanical, making religious organizations too reactive to their environments, it should also be recognized that one of the reasons organizations exist in the first place is to *manage* resources and *plan* for uncertainty. Churches do not respond blindly to changes in their neighborhoods; they garner finances in good times so they can relocate if they have to. Or they try to anticipate changes in pressing needs and issues and thus be ready to provide, for example, day-care programs at one time and services to the elderly at another. This tendency to manage and plan, we can note here in passing, also generates a kind of rationality that may or may not be conducive to the images of sacredness those organizations are actually attempting to instill in the public arena.

Management, Control, Power

We have now moved well into the seamy side of cultural production. Artists attracted to their professions because of pure aesthetic values hold these practical matters in high disdain; people of faith are sure to dispel them for the same reasons. But we must move even further into this murky domain if we are to understand what lies beneath the lofty and sometimes not so lofty expressions of the sacred we see in public life. It is one thing to acknowledge that religious organizations, like all organizations, must bend with the times or be broken by them; it is quite another to suggest that the leaders of religious organizations intentionally scheme to make their fiefdoms more successful, that power games are played in the halls of God, and that mechanisms are put in place to keep people out as well as to draw them in. Yet anyone who has ever served on a church committee or talked candidly with members of the clergy knows these are the harsh realities of religious life.

One aspect of these realities that has probably received less attention than it merits (management and power are increasingly recognized in discussions of church leadership) is the way in which any cultural organization protects itself by generating products that in turn become the basis for cultural exclusion. In the worlds of art it has not been cynics alone who have shown how modern art restricts its own audience by being so abstract that only those with requisite training can appreciate it. The same tendency has been seen in the professions; whether medicine or law or science, ever more specialized training is required, thus keeping the pool of eligible entrants sufficiently small to ensure the high status, salaries, and access to resources of those already in these professions. By the same token the consumers of "high" or elite culture often engage in similar practices of cultural exclusion, by, for example, talking about expensive vacations or experiences at private boarding schools that necessarily exclude lower-income persons from participating in the discussion. In contrast, religious organizations ascribe to the values of openness, inclusion, acceptance, and love. Can anything like the cultural exclusion that occurs in other organizations take place here?

Let us consider this question, not by giving a quick answer one way or the other but by using some of the arguments we have already considered about producers, consumers, and competition. As noted earlier, consumers of cultural products often exercise great control over the nature of these products, especially when it is a "buyer's market." In most churches a market of this type would seem to prevail. Usually there are a number of competing churches, and their ability to do anything depends very much on their members' being loyal and contributing resources; moreover, religious freedom in this context means that people can vote with their feet if they do not like what they receive from a particular church. Pastors worry aloud that saying the wrong thing may cause a substantial share of their parishioners to leave, and parishioners sometimes report with pride that they have done just that.

There must also be some restrictions on this sort of consumer power, however. Colleges also compete for students, who can shop around and even transfer if they become unhappy, and yet students do not determine what colleges teach. Why not? Partly the answer lies in the concept of isomorphism that we have already considered. To protect themselves from completely open competition in which consumers dictate the rules, organizations become similar to one another. They all produce the same thing, and this defines what a legitimate institution is, including what a consumer may legitimately expect of an institution. Thus, if a student wants to listen to rock music all day, college is not (or may not be) the place to do it.

For it to be effective, however, isomorphism depends on organizations' having a certifiable product; that is, they must be able to produce something that people want badly enough to put up with whatever else the institution may impose. For example, students apparently want a college degree, one that is worth something, badly enough to put up with all the other rules and activities colleges impose on them. The key of course is the ability to certify something. A college degree might be obtained from a mail-order catalog, but it would be worthless, even if someone had learned a lot in the process, because colleges hold a monopoly over the right to certify one's education. The older, or more prestigious, or more populated with Nobel Prize winners the faculty is, the more a particular college can provide that kind of cultural legitimacy.

This, then, is where cultural exclusion comes into the picture. You might be able to find spirituality anywhere, but you have to go to certain churches to get it certified, that is, to see that people whom you respect and admire believe the same way you do and, moreover, are willing to confer their blessings on you for believing the way you do. You can make up a belief about the supernatural, but if you wonder whether your belief makes any sense, you have to check it out with other people.

In seeking confirmation from other people, you may be content to discover that the guy who pumps gas at the local station thinks you have a neat idea, especially if you are a station attendant yourself. Yet you may be concerned that your idea is not subject to some silly fallacy that others much more thoughtful than you had refuted long ago. Or you might be even more curious to know if someone you really respect and admire, like the person who runs the bank, thinks the same way you do. You might of course ask yourself why you should even care about something as crass as what the banker thinks. Since there is a certain holistic quality about our self-identities, however, you may not want to hold some belief that is just completely deviant, and if you are a banker yourself, you may be especially concerned that your religious views also have standing in the banking community (how often do college professors hold beliefs they feel are good and proper for professors to hold?). In short you want to hold your beliefs but be respectable too.

The obvious answer is to attend the Ralph Lauren Country Club Church, where you can be affirmed in your faith by the rich and powerful people in your community. Seeing that they believe as you do helps assure you that your views about God are not those one might find in the *National Enquirer*. This is a genuine service the church can provide, and it is of course one of the ways in which religion becomes public and an important means by which public religion is certified. Nor are churches the only institutions that do this. Colleges and universities engage in much the same business, taking young people just when they are making up their minds about life and telling them it is respectable to think in certain ways.

How then does a church control what it believes and who believes it enough that people want to go there to gain its certification? This is where specialization can help. There may be few deep theological differences between any two or three churches in town, but there will probably be a division of labor in the kinds of certification they provide. A few churches may do everything in such impeccably good taste that nobody with high-status aspirations feels his or her own tastes are being compromised. Other churches may provide extensive Bible and church history classes, so people feel they have really learned what the experts have to say. Still others may provide such a good program for the children that parents are willing to endure almost anything for their sake. Other possibilities for developing a specialized niche include grandstanding a dynamic preacher who says things that tickle the imagination; being so close by and demanding so little that people can get whatever they need at minimal cost to themselves; debunking all cult figures and charlatans in other churches who may provide competition; excluding people from good standing unless they can pray like Elijah; giving assurance that people are really saved (or have the spirit of God) and that everyone else there has been too; and playing up ethnic roots. Cultural exclusion, then, consists of defining something as a good and limiting people's access to it, thereby making it a scarce commodity. An example would be defining an Ivy League degree as a good and limiting the number of students who can get one so its value remains high. In religion eternal salvation has traditionally been the standard scarce good, but its scarcity has been greatly reduced by churches that have made it easy to get or that have suggested people do not need to get it at all. In adapting to secular society, churches have thus found other ways to practice cultural exclusion. It is not at all farfetched to imagine there are people who believe it is good to be able to associate with bankers in the community who, like themselves, are also good people and indeed may do favors for people they know. Since gaining access to these bankers is not easy nowadays because they are locked away in their homes and private clubs most of the time, it is especially advantageous if there is a church in town, like the Ralph Lauren Country Club Church, that some of these bankers attend. In addition to anything else it may offer, this church has a valuable good. It also has a control problem, though. How is it possible to make this good scarce? If people of lower standing in the community can gain access to these bankers any time they please just by attending the same church, pretty soon the bankers are likely to feel demeaned and leave. The church probably cannot get away with posting a sign saying "Bankers only welcome here." Nor will its control problem be solved by teaching some sort of correct theological belief that anyone could understand and accept.

What is needed is a combination of an esoteric definition of correct beliefs and subtle behavioral cues. One of the best ways to serve up a correct belief system that cannot be understood too widely is, first, to assert that we do not believe what everyone else believes and, then, refuse to make it very clear what we do believe and sprinkle our teachings with references to esoteric historical, philosophical, and theological sources of wisdom. The best behavioral cues are ones that show we only reward people who act like bankers. For example, give people who have expertise in handling money the top committee positions and choose them to take up the morning offering or read the verses and prayers. Presumably people who attend will want and admire the sophisticated ways of these leaders, but those who do not have it or do not even come close to having it will feel uncomfortable or unrewarded enough to go away. (How else can we explain the persistence over generations of some denominations with high-status memberships?)

This is perhaps an extreme example, and most religious leaders would probably deny they practice any kind of deliberate cultural exclusion. Yet there does seem to be evidence that some denominations are more comfortable occupying ever-smaller niches in the social environment than attempting to broaden their base by examining their own, perhaps nondeliberate, exclusiveness. Nor, from the standpoint of cultural production theory, is it terribly surprising that this should be the case. Public religion is always created by and for specific publics. For these publics to have any distinct identity they must maintain their boundaries, buttressing the scarcity of their valued goods by limiting access to these goods. The only question is whether these boundaries define the goods these organizations hope to project into the public arena or they reinforce messages that are unintended and contrary to the sacred.

Organizational Culture and the Sacred

A final topic that must be considered in introducing the cultural production perspective is the extent to which organizations actually produce culture that is about *themselves*. Let us consider the following distinction: some cultural products in actuality have very little to do with the specific organizations that produce them (for example, at the organization where I am employed, mathematical formulas are produced but so are books of Chinese poetry, jazz concerts, and weddings); other cultural products include overt or thinly disguised references to their producing organizations (for example, Princeton's alumni magazine or the references I have just made to my own institution). Religious organizations contribute to the sacred by producing sermons, tracts, and commentaries about the sacred itself, but they also produce vast quantities of information about themselves, such as congregational histories, the annual reports of denominations, and even news reports about the goings and comings of their leaders.

Self-referential material of this kind, to give it a name, is a natural output of any organization because of the internal monitoring, managing, and planning that we have already discussed. The relevance of this material for understanding public religion is, first, that some organizational energy is also likely to be expended keeping the two kinds of information separate and, second, that these efforts are never likely to be (nor should they be) completely successful, and public religion will thus consist of not only ideas about the sacred but also images and projections of the human vessels in which the sacred is articulated. The efforts to keep the two separate used to be performed fairly effectively, at least by the more authoritarian religious structures that could simply build walls of secrecy around their financial dealings and internal squabbles. In the United States such efforts are still made at least in token ways (business meetings are restricted to active members and held at different times than church services are, inner circles of lay leaders rule on sensitive issues, and higher officials shield themselves from public view), but these efforts are seldom effective, partly because the mass media's appetite for religious scandals has grown rapaciously and partly because religious organizations themselves have become more democratically oriented. As a result, public religion may be more what is known by the public about religious organizations than it is imagery and conviction about the sacred itself.

We return, then, to the fact that public religion is never purely what its most devout advocates would like it to be. Because it is produced by human organizations, it is subject to all the failings of these organizations. For the same reason, much of its *content* is shaped by these organizations as well. Not only is public religion the product of its social context but its context becomes a significant feature of its content as well.

2

Congregations

The congregation is typically the level of social organization at which religious commitment is conceived of as being most influential. If it does not affect the lives of individuals by drawing them into an intimate community, encouraging them to worship, and providing them and their children with instruction, religion is unlikely to be of any lasting personal or social significance.

In the West the congregation is also virtually synonymous with the history of Christianity. The early Christians met in homes because they did not have public places of worship and in many instances would have been subject to persecution had their meetings been held in public. Gradually these small, informal meetings grew in size, and congregations became the common modes of gathering for Christians as the new faith spread from city to city. When Christianity became the official religion of the Roman Empire in the fourth century, congregations were generally formalized, with established geographic distinctions, leading to the system of churches and parishes that dominated Europe until the Protestant Reformation in the sixteenth century and still characterizes the Roman Catholic church.

Although the medieval parish varied considerably in the size of population and territory it encompassed, a typical parish was generally small enough to provide people with a sense of primary attachment to their communities. In rural areas the church was usually within convenient walking distance, and its bells could be heard by most of the people in its vicinity. In the towns rapid population growth sometimes made the church a less intimate place of worship,

but urban residents generally attended churches in their neighborhood or section of the city and were often related to other parishioners and the priests.

The medieval parish bound people together through a complex
set of rituals and activities. In addition to the fact that they were
probably related to the priest, the people were often attached to a
landlord who controlled appointments to the priesthood and whose
donations played the largest role in maintaining the church facilities. Sacraments of marriage and baptism bound villagers together
in systems of godparentage and sponsorship. The holy days of the
church calendar corresponded to community festivals and marked
times for planting, harvesting, and other economic activities. Patron
saints often identified the community with its ancestors, and some
records indicate that prayers, fasting, and various acts that would
now be considered superstitious played a prominent role in the daily
lives of individuals and families.

The Protestant Reformation swept away many of the relics, super-
stitions, and clerical offices of the medieval church but replaced them
with congregations that depended even more strongly on local community ties. Preaching in Latin was replaced by preaching in the
language of the people, the laity partook of both the bread and the
wine during the celebration of communion, and pastors were often
selected and supported by members of the local congregation. With
the exception of various Anabaptist groups that were often severely
persecuted because of their nonconformity, congregations in most
areas typically took the form laid down for them by higher authorities as part of the state church arrangements that prevailed in most of
the Protestant countries. There was therefore little room for choice
as far as which congregation to attend.

It was the Protestant congregational form that the first settlers
brought to the American colonies a century after the Reformation.
Preaching was still very much the centerpiece of the congregations'
activities, but typically the church was also integrated into the entire life of a local settlement. Moral order was maintained through
the disciplinary activities of the church, and being a person in good
standing in the community often meant being a person with staunch
religious scruples as well. Although broader coordinating bodies
existed to govern the activities of particular congregations, the early
settlements were often able to institute a high degree of congrega-

tional autonomy because of their geographic distance from parent bodies in Europe or other congregations in the colonies themselves.

As the American population gradually increased and spread westward into new territories, congregations continued to play an integral role in these communities. Many areas were settled by immigrants who shared the same religious convictions and for this reason were able to form new congregations from the outset. Other congregations came into being, especially during the nineteenth century, as a result of itinerant missionaries and revivalists, who traveled from community to community preaching to the settlers and encouraging them to form churches. The most distinctive feature of this period was that in towns, cities, and even in many rural areas congregations representing several different faiths or denominational traditions now existed in the proximity of one another.

Only toward the end of the nineteenth century did the typical congregation begin taking on the more expanded functions associated with churches today. Among the first activities to be added beyond the usual Sunday morning (and sometimes Sunday evening) preaching services were educational activities and prayer meetings. Sunday school classes for children, and later for adults, and an evening gathering of some kind in midweek for prayer or Bible study gradually came to be the accepted standard. Various benevolent activities and societies to assist in the support of missionary programs also became part of the typical congregation's functions.

At the beginning of the twentieth century churches existed in nearly every community in the United States, and despite the enormous growth in population that had taken place during the preceding century, a larger proportion of the population appeared to be involved in local congregations than ever before. Most congregations, moreover, were still sufficiently small, generally averaging fewer than a hundred adult members, that genuine interaction among the congregants could take place.

The changes that religious congregations have undergone in the United States during the twentieth century have been more dramatic than at virtually any other time in history. From an initial membership of fewer than a hundred, the typical congregation has grown to more than three hundred members. Diversity has mushroomed because of increases in the number and variety of Protestant denominations, huge increases in the numbers of Catholics and Jews, and, more recently, increases in Muslims, Buddhists, and a variety of sects and cults. The functions served by the typical congregation have also expanded enormously: a much enlarged range of educational offerings, fellowship groups defined by gender and age categories, special ministries, counseling, visitation, community service projects, and study groups of all kinds. Congregations are also embedded in much larger, formal administrative networks and must compete with religious organizations based on different social arrangements. Yet the congregation retains many of its traditional forms and much of its historic vitality.

With more than 300,000 local congregations in which approximately two out of every three adults nationwide claim to be members, American religion is still very much organized at the congregational level. These are the primary bases in which public religion is produced. They account for several million sermons each year; put on millions of services in which singing, the sacraments, and other acts of worship are made public; sponsor enormous numbers of Sunday school classes, adult forums, Bible studies, and discussion groups in which religious sentiments become open for collective consideration; and produce any number of community services, newspaper stories, and informal interaction that contribute to the shaping of American public religion.

The Perplexing Familiarity of Congregations

The history of local congregations is on the whole quite familiar, and their presence along the main boulevards of virtually every town makes them even more commonplace. Every Protestant denomination is divided into local congregations, Catholic parishes function as congregations, Jewish synagogues are often referred to as congregations, and even something like a Black Muslim group is probably going to be organized as a congregation. But what is a congregation?

The largest congregation in the world is said to be in Korea. It numbers 700,000 members. Is that a congregation? In the United States some churches have memberships of 20,000 and can perhaps seat as many as 5,000 at a time. Are these congregations? Or, at the other extreme, how about a group of a dozen neighbors who meet regularly in someone's living room for prayer, singing, and personal testimonies? Is this group a congregation?

If variations in size cause problems in deciding when something is legitimately considered a congregation, so does terminology that overlaps to a great extent with our usage of the word. A "church" can be anything from the Roman Catholic church or the Church of Jesus Christ of Latter-day Saints, both organized on an international scale, to the First Baptist Church located at the corner of Main and Elm. Often *church* and *congregation* are used interchangeably, but the latter is a more precise term because it refers to something that usually exists at a single geographic location. I say "usually" because we can think of a congregation, perhaps like the example of a neighborhood group, that meets in several different places because it does not have a facility of its own. This possibility points up the additional fact that a congregation is a social entity, not a building or a place. We can imagine a single facility housing two congregations, for example, a church building used by Seventh-Day Adventists on Saturdays and Presbyterians on Sundays.

To understand what a congregation is, we must also distinguish it from the word *community*, which has become popular in religious circles in recent years. When pastors announce to those assembled at their churches on Sunday morning that they hope they will find community, they do so advisedly. Community, in this usage, implies a supportive set of interpersonal relationships that forge a common bond of identity and caring among people. It requires interaction, give and take. A congregation in contrast connotes something more akin to a gathering or an assembly than to a community. To congregate means literally to come together. People can be part of a congregation without knowing each other or interacting on a personal level. At many medium-sized churches, for example, space limitations require more than one worship service each Sunday morning; the people who attend one may seldom even see those who attend the other, so they are not part of the same community, and yet they are all members of the same congregation.

What differentiates a congregation from a mere assembly, such as the audience that gathers in the park for a spring concert, is that there is also a sense of corporate identity attached to a congregation. In fact, most congregations in the United States enjoy the legal status of being corporate entities according to state law, and as such they must have a name, an address, a charter or statement of purpose, and a set of bylaws. Even when these legal requirements have not been met, as might be the case in a small church that meets in people's homes, it is the sense that here is something of a social nature with a regular existence and identity of its own that is decisive.

The corporateness of congregations comes about partly through time. This is why a sporadic gathering in the park is an assembly but not a congregation. If it met every week at the same time and in the same place and if many of the same people attended each time, a sense of corporateness might gradually develop. They would begin thinking of themselves as the "Wednesday evening park crowd" or something similar. We should not, however, assume that corporateness merely evolves by itself, as a kind of idea that springs to fruition in the heads of the individuals involved. Corporateness is generally a conferred identity. Sometimes it is conferred by the state, as in the case of a legal entity being formed. In religion it is often conferred by some other agency "from above," as it were, such as a bishop who comes to town and decrees that the fellowship meeting in the town hall will henceforth be called a Methodist church. It may also be an identity conferred by the people upon themselves, for example, by a leader who declares that the group should think of itself as a group or by popular consensus that emerges around some common name or stated purpose or symbol.

The point of this exercise is to show that congregations are by definition part of public religion. For them to exist, they must have some corporate identity, and this identity must in some way be public, especially among the members themselves but usually to some outside authority or wider public as well. Having a church building often helps create this public identity, but it clearly is not essential. Having community in the form of a membership that cares for one another and interacts socially in a deep and intensive way may also help, but it too is not absolutely essential. Certainly a congregation still exists if some particular member fails to show up at a given service. The congregation even exists if it declares itself to be on summer vacation and nobody shows up at all. This is also why we can legitimately speak of congregations with twenty people or twenty thousand people. They will face very different problems and be very different in the activities they can pursue, but either group can define itself as a single congregation.

The Resources to Be Public

If, by definition, congregations are public, they nevertheless do a lot more than simply exist to produce cultural goods and services that contribute to the shaping of public religion. Opinion polls asking people why they attend their particular church and what they like best about it usually find that personal spiritual growth looms high. People also attend for a variety of other personal reasons, such as comfort when they are feeling depressed and support when they are lonely or experiencing personal trauma. In addition, congregations have typically provided services that augment or substitute for the nuclear family, such as inexpensive child care during the Sunday brunch period, dating and mating services for teenagers, and small fellowship groups for the divorced, separated, and widowed. To maintain a public witness in their communities, congregations have to draw people in by providing this array of personal services.

To clergy and other congregation leaders, *resources* is likely to imply, above all else, finances. Finances, in turn, depend on the willingness of members to give voluntarily. The voluntariness of these gifts has in fact increased over the years as religious teachings have come to deemphasize such quasi-coercive practices as pew rents, membership fees, and literal interpretations of the tithe. At present, giving to religious causes still occurs primarily at the congregation level, and compared with giving to other charitable organizations, religious giving ranks high both in overall terms and as a percentage of personal income. As a result of expanded programs on the part of churches themselves and growing competition from secular service organizations, the importance of giving has increased, making church finances a more problematic issue. The expansion of church programs has taken place over a relatively long period, dating back well into the nineteenth century, and is one of the principal reasons for the stewardship sermons and pledge campaigns that are now common in most congregations. By the end of the nineteenth century churches were already involved in a wide variety of service activities and ministries, including foreign and domestic missions, church construction and renovation, poor relief, hospitals, and clerical recruitment, all of which incurred greater financial obligations. These activities have continued throughout the twentieth century. At the same time, pressures to maintain and upgrade these programs have increasingly come from the outside, as community and secular agencies compete with churches to be the bearers of mercy and good deeds. Giving to educational institutions; national charities, such as United Way and Red Cross; leisure and hobby groups, such as Little League Baseball; and social and environmental causes has increased dramatically, relative to religious organizations, as a proportion of total voluntary giving.

Financial resources is one of the areas in which congregations' own needs often interfere with the public messages they wish to convey. Sentiment in the public at large still runs deep about the need to distinguish sharply between God and mammon. People who are otherwise quite materialistic in their own lives want their clergy and churches to be preoccupied with heavenly things and express disdain toward religious groups that seem too interested in money. What is less often clear to the public is that financial pressures have also made congregation leaders themselves more concerned about running a financially efficient operation, even when efficiency may conflict with meeting higher aims, such as nourishing the soul and healing the sick. Moreover, these same concerns have sometimes been heightened by large donors' attaching strings to their gifts, thereby exercising inordinate control over the direction congregations' programs may take.

The other resource on which local congregations continue to depend heavily is voluntary contributions of time. Research on the extent of voluntary service indicates that it is still extensive, that it accounts for a much greater share of congregations' overall programs than does the paid effort of clergy, and that church members give far more of their time in voluntary service of all kinds than do people unaffiliated with congregations. Virtually all of the teaching, visitation, and committee work associated with churches is still provided voluntarily, and even something as professionally led as the Sunday morning preaching service requires vast contributions of volunteer effort, from ushering and arranging for flowers to making coffee, providing child care, and singing in the choir.

Less visible on a week-to-week basis, but equally vital, are the political resources on which the functioning of local congregations depend. At one time people interested in forming themselves as a congregation probably got together, called a pastor, and put up a building, with little consultation required from the outside. The prevalence of neighborhood churches in older communities attests to the degree of localism that was involved in most instances. Now congregations must meet zoning requirements, deal with greedy land developers and planning boards serving the interests of these developers, and attend to everything from construction codes to fair labor practices to health and safety standards. Indicating the power of these arrangements, maps of congregations in newer suburban communities often show them located along highways, near busy intersections, and well away from the high-priced land that developers retain for their most prized construction projects. Part of the public religion projected by these congregations has also arisen simply from their need to testify before municipal boards, not about the Lord but about drainage, sewers, and parking facilities.

In the United States congregations have adapted relatively well to their environments as a result of constitutional restrictions that prevent government agencies from interfering more with religious affairs and because of the sustained efforts of religious leaders to maintain these guarantees. Other countries with weaker traditions of religious involvement and greater intermingling of religious and governmental influences have witnessed a long-term erosion in the strength and vitality of local congregations.

Some of the continuing success of congregations in securing the resources needed to make public their vision of the sacred is attributable to the fact that these organizations have not only filled but also created a distinct niche in the social environment. For all the competition, including the proverbial temptations of Sunday morning golf outings and late Saturday evening baseball innings, congregations remain the one place where people can actually come together to engage collectively in worship. Of course hymns could be sung privately and inspiration can be obtained by reading a good book of poetry, but the sense of unity *and* devotion to the divine is something that can only be found in houses of worship. This is a niche that is less easily replaced or paved over by other preoccupations because it constantly re-creates and replenishes itself. Were the function of congregations simply to provide people with occasions to worship, worship might become occasional indeed, happening only on high holy days or at times of major life transitions. But congregations also use the time people come to worship to good advantage, reminding them that they *must* come together to worship if they are true believers, that *this* is the place where they are "especially welcome" to come together, and that a good way to express their worship is by contributing to the offering.

The rivalry among competing congregations encourages this sort of sweet persuasion, yet it also leads to the efforts, about which we have reflected, of churches to specialize their ministries. Until well into the twentieth century congregations specialized primarily on the basis of denominational divisions. One town of any size usually meant one Presbyterian church, one Methodist church, one Baptist church, and one Catholic church (or some other combination). People knew the liturgy was a little different in each of these churches. They also knew that social, economic, and cultural divisions corresponded to these differences: Presbyterians were the town's doctors and lawyers, Methodists included the middling ranks of shopkeepers and farmers, Baptists were more likely to be the poorer people, and Catholics were recent immigrants. As the town grew, more churches of wider denominational diversity were added (Lutherans, Nazarenes, Pentecostalists), and some of the established congregations spun off new ones still differentiated by social factors; for example, the Second Presbyterian Church was probably populated by younger people who lived in a new section of town and managed the new plant in town instead of being doctors and lawyers. This sort of specialization meant that congregations could reduce the level of direct competition and provide activities that fit the particular interests and life-styles of their members. Indeed, this system often worked so well that congregations were able to coexist amicably and even work together harmoniously on community service projects, such as banning liquor (or keeping out Jews).

Over the past half-century many of these traditional modes of specialization have broken down, forcing congregations to be more creative in differentiating themselves from one another. Increased mobility, more marriages crossing denominational lines, greater similarities among the major faiths in income and education levels, an erosion of ethnic identities, and even a weakening of official teachings about the distinctiveness of particular traditions all contributed to the declining influence of earlier forms of specialization. One of the most significant ways in which congregations now set themselves off from one another is their size and thus the menu of activities that can be provided. The major types are the small church (of two kinds), the family church, and the megachurch.

The small church usually consists of fewer than a hundred members. In the nineteenth century a congregation of that size would have been average, but at the end of the twentieth century it is well below average. Small churches can generally be divided into two categories: the neighborhood church and the intentional church. The neighborhood church is more likely to be an older, well-established congregation that reached the capacity of its building or did not grow beyond its immediate neighborhood; it is often a congregation that has declined in total membership because of changes in its neighborhood (children move away and newcomers either remain unchurched or drive to larger churches outside the neighborhood). The intentional church is likely to be a newer congregation, often a mission church that has been started in a new neighborhood and is hoping to become larger with time, or a group that wants to remain small for a variety of reasons.

The advantages of the small church (which are also the reasons some groups give for wanting to remain small) are the intimacy that can develop when the entire congregation can be acquainted with one another, a focus on such "basics" as preaching and Bible study, the chance to retain or uphold some particular tradition or doctrine (such as the traditional ties of the neighborhood or the belief that only a certain style of singing is appropriate), and freedom from the added effort and expense that would be required to attract larger numbers, engage in more activities, and construct larger facilities.

The family church is usually a congregation of between two hundred and three hundred members, making it closer to the average for all congregations in the United States today. Actual membership in some family churches may range as high as five hundred or more, but the number of active participants is seldom more than half that number. As an average-sized congregation, the family church (also sometimes called the "program" church) can provide a broader range of activities than the small church can, but it must still choose carefully among these activities. It therefore often focuses on those programs that are most likely to attract the modal segment of the population, which generally consists of married people with children (from whence the term "family church" derives). Worship services are likely to include special times for children, child care is generally provided, and other activities are likely to include education programs for children, youth groups, and classes or fellowship groups for married people or for age- and gender-related special interests. If more than one clergy member is employed, the most likely additions in the family church are a youth pastor and an education director. Family churches, like smaller churches, may have a strong neighborhood base but usually draw parishioners from a wider area, often because of a particular preaching style or an attractive program for families.

The megachurch is a congregation of at least a thousand members, and it may range as high as ten to twenty thousand members in some communities. Because of its size the megachurch is able to provide a wide variety of activities and programs, including those geared toward not only the conventional middle- or working-class family but also populations with special needs and interests, such as single adults, homosexuals, the handicapped, the poor, those with special talents in music, college students, or any number of more specialized groups. To operate these activities, megachurches require large facilities, and their staffs may include administrators, choir directors, chaplains, and a host of other specialists, as well as pastors. These churches tend to be concentrated in metropolitan areas, attract people who are willing to commute considerable distances for specialized programs, and have less to do with local neighborhoods.

These varieties of congregations generally play quite different roles in contributing to the public expression of the sacred. The small neighborhood church, because of its traditional ties to the neighborhood itself, generally takes an interest in local community affairs and may encourage its members to be involved in service efforts, such as work in the volunteer fire company, visitation at a local nursing home, or membership in civic organizations. Not attempting to expand its functions, it seldom comes into conflict with zoning laws or finds itself in confrontation with public authorities at the local level, although such conflicts can arise with particular vehemence when the neighborhood itself is threatened by, for example, changing racial or ethnic composition. The small intentional church, usually newer to its host community, is generally less involved in wider public efforts in the community itself and indeed may withdraw largely into its own membership. Its public activities are more likely to

occur through larger organizations, such as environmental or anti-
abortion movements. Some small intentional congregations, for example, have become quite active in prolife efforts or have pushed for
nuclear freeze legislation. As congregations, however, their public
witness is chiefly through the individual lives of their members. The
family church has long been the mainstay of public religion, perpetuating traditional moral and familial values, providing facilities
for scout meetings, and reinforcing the faith of community leaders.
Clergy and lay leaders in these churches are often prominent in their
communities and may be actively involved in volunteer work. How
active these congregations may be in promoting public issues beyond those of the conventional family is likely to depend largely on
the clergy. Megachurches have in recent decades become much more
prominent influences on public religion. Their visibility is sometimes heightened by television or radio ministries, their economic
and political power in a particular metropolitan region may be considerable, and their pastors may even have connections with national
centers of power. That they often incorporate minority interests into
their memberships also increases the likelihood of their speaking
out in ways that may challenge taken-for-granted social and political norms.

Despite the differences that separate these types of congregations,
they all adapt to their social environments partly through isomorphic structures of the kind we considered in the last chapter. The
vast differences in size and activities do not prevent us from referring to all of them as "churches" or from recognizing that they are
different from most other organizations. How is this possible, and
what does it tell us about public religion? It is possible largely because the social environment itself is deeply institutionalized; that
is, churches are not just buildings set in clearings in the wilderness
but are organizations constituted by a dense system of legal and cultural norms. Even before there is a building or a sizable number of
adherents, a church is constituted by the charter and by-laws that
it must file with the state to operate and gain protection from taxa-
tion. Churches themselves are also quick to apply their norms to any
newcomers who might be engaged in religious activities. Something
that is not perceived to be a church is often termed a cult, and this
designation usually means a group to be disliked and distrusted.

Although there are some exceptions, congregations also come to resemble one another because they are in business not to invent the sacred but to encourage people to *discover* it. The difference is significant. The avenue of discovery may be unique for each individual, but what is discovered has an existence independent of the seeker's imagination. That existence generally includes some implicit assumptions at the very least. For example, the God that people in most congregations attempt to discover is assumed to be a being described in the books these congregations provide in their pews, a being who likes to hear people sing certain songs that have been part of traditional worship services for years and years, and one who tolerates (perhaps even appreciates) people trying to address him or her (usually him) with certain formulaic prayers. What earns other groups the designation of cult is that they are not content to abide by these norms; instead of discovering the sacred, they may even try to invent it.

Activities and Publics

In anticipation of what we will have to say about hierarchies and special interests, it is important to recognize here that all congregations, from the smallest to the largest, are multipurpose organizations that attempt to appeal to a mixed, and sometimes confused, variety of publics. The multiple purposes served by congregations are most clear in megachurches, where these functions are likely to be pursued by separate programs under the supervision of specialized staff members. Even in the small neighborhood church the congregation exists for a variety of reasons. Its stated purpose may be to worship God, thereby giving public expression to the sacred, and yet its clergy and members would likely recognize other purposes as well: to help celebrate the good times experienced by the congregants, to bury and grieve their dead and comfort their survivors, to come together for fun and fellowship, to study new ideas and maintain their knowledge of basic scriptural teachings, perhaps to help a needy family, or to provide a clean basement to which people in the neighborhood can come to hear a piano recital. The congregation is also supposed to be open to people with different interests, personalities, and viewpoints. To be sure, norms may be invoked to keep some people out, at least by making them feel uncomfortable, yet deviance is often tolerated that could not be countenanced in most other organizations.

The multipurpose nature of congregations is extremely important for understanding their contribution to the public arena. More specialized organizations often make a very focused contribution and bracket from consideration anything deemed to fall outside their purview. A soft-drink manufacturer, for example, expends billions each year on advertising for a single purpose: to get consumers to buy more of its product. One can imagine that the behind-the-scenes discussions from which those advertisements emanate do not consider many of the basic values on which a society depends (such as love, peace, justice, and democracy). To the extent that these are brought in, they are included in an interesting reversal of means and ends: Product X is not the means to attaining love and happiness; love and happiness are the means to sell Product X. One can also imagine that if a participant in these behind-the-scenes discussions wanted to spend the day thinking about peace and justice, that person would soon be dismissed. The point is that specialized organizations exist because they have already decided on a basic goal, and even if that goal is laudable, their focus will be on finding the most efficient means of attaining that objective rather than deliberating its worth relative to a variety of other objectives. Even when the organization is "diversified," as it might be in producing both telephones and toothpaste, its underlying goal (profitability) is clearly in place.

Congregations are different. Although the norms of bureaucratic efficiency can subvert their ability to consider the widest range of human values, congregations are often compelled by their very nature to do so. This is not, as philosophers have sometimes argued, because something in the nature of the sacred itself, as a high value, forces consideration of all lower-order values. It is because the sacred is not clearly defined and the ways of addressing it are not narrowly delineated. Worship can be defined as corporate prayer and hymn singing, for example, but it can also be understood in terms of working to achieve justice for the oppressed or engaging in a fellowship dinner that is "honoring to God." Congregants may be content to focus on the most efficient means of putting on a chicken dinner, but it is more likely their deliberations will include questions about the relationships among basic values themselves, whether these be advocacy versus consensus, God versus human obligations, or doctrine versus behavior. The congregation, in making itself open to a diverse group of individuals and in attempting to serve a variety of functions, is thus an exceptional forum in which debate over fundamental public values can take place.

The range of relevant considerations is also broadened by the fact that congregations are oriented toward multiple and overlapping publics. To be more precise, let us imagine the content of a typical sermon, since it may be that this more than anything else constitutes the actual discourse emerging on a regular basis from the congregation. The sermon is likely to have the assembled audience in mind as its primary public, yet it is also likely to treat this audience not as a unitary entity but as a series of subgroups whose boundaries may spill over to a much wider public: those of you who are educated, those of you who are feeling depressed, those of you who are uncertain what to believe. By virtue of the inclusiveness of the theology underlying the sermon itself, there is likely to be an even broader message: we are part of the church universal, so what we say here is congruent with what is being said in other churches; and we are to be salt to the earth, so our public is indeed the entire world. It is therefore important to use several languages, that is, several registers that bring into conjunction with one another the various standards of evaluation that may exist in these registers.

This is how congregations may, in theory, contribute to the public expression of collective values. That practice itself is often less inclusive and more restrictive can be understood better in reference to this theoretical potential. If religious discourse is indeed subject to bringing up a wide range of conceptions of the good, then it should be no surprise that congregations find ways to limit these possibilities. Norms of communal harmony and of organizational effectiveness require them to do so. A church might call two pastors with widely differing views and have them battle it out every week, but in most instances this is not the preferred approach. A single pastor articulates some values largely at the exclusion of others. Even a diverse congregation is likely to communicate subtle behavioral cues that deter members of other backgrounds and persuasions from attending. We thus expect to find the fullest expression of public values in the larger pluralism of congregations that exist in the wider society.

How Congregations Manifest the Sacred

What then is sacred about what congregations do? An odd question to ask, perhaps, since churches are so explicitly engaged in the production of the sacred. Yet we need to step back from the taken-for-granted realities of churches as producers of the sacred and try to see what sort of sacredness is being generated and what makes us regard this as sacred.

It is possible to give a simple answer to these questions that, while completely unsatisfactory in itself, provides a useful starting place. Congregations are able to define whatever they do as having something to do with the sacred, this answer suggests, because people are culturally conditioned to think of congregations in this way. In short, we *expect* churches to be in the business of producing the sacred.

This answer is deeper than it may appear to be at first glance because it points to the important fact that we do not for the most part invent the sacred from scratch. The situation is not one where nobody has ever thought of the idea of worshipping God until some organization calling itself a church comes along and tries to convince everyone that this is a reasonable idea. Especially in a society like ours, where the sacred has a long history of association with religious institutions, congregations can get away with a lot just by linking themselves to this history.

They cannot, however, get away with just anything, and this is where we must try to understand a bit better what it takes to make something sacred. We can take a basic insight from Émile Durkheim's work on the sacred in primitive societies as a clue. Durkheim suggested that the sacred gains that identity, among other things, by being ritually set apart from the ordinary world of everyday life. In the primitive case people sometimes had to fast for several days or engage in many purifying rituals before they could participate in a sacred ceremony. These activities drew a sharp boundary between the profane and the sacred. In our time such rituals would seem excessive, but religious congregations continue to be set off from everyday life in some of these ways. It helps greatly, for example, for congregations to have their own buildings; people meeting in homes or school auditoriums have to find other ways to turn these into sacred places at the right moment. It also helps, despite all the pretensions that may arise, for congregations to construct their buildings to look different from homes, schools, and office buildings. Steeples and stained glass have their purpose. It even helps for people to dress up or for choirs and clergy to wear robes that set them apart from the everyday world. These distinctions draw cultural boundaries, and they work only in conjunction with the fact, as we observed initially, that people *expect* something religious to go on in these places. (Restroom signs draw boundaries, too, but that by itself does not create a sacred space.)

We should note of course that even this much understanding of the sacred suggests some worrisome possibilities about the future of the sacred. When people dressed in overalls all week, it was probably helpful in identifying the sacred to put on suits and ties; now that many wear professional garb, it might be necessary to invent special clothes to wear to church. Should building codes rule out the use of stained glass and steeples, some other distinctive form of architecture would need to be developed. Meeting in homes and public auditoriums may be a good way to save on mortgage payments, but it may be necessary to put up temporary banners to identify these places as houses of worship.

To understand why *congregations* may be especially good at producing the sacred, we also need to draw a second insight from Durkheim. His view of the sacred linked it closely to the sense of power that derives from doing things with others — being in their presence and doing things collectively with them. People in modern societies persist in reporting they have been in touch with the sacred while fishing (which probably has something to do with the separation between fishing and everyday life), but more continue to feel God's presence when they are gathered with others in corporate acts of worship. Congregations are the places where that can happen.

Increasingly, though, the most powerful experiences of being with other people are in public auditoriums and stadiums rather than in church buildings. Does this not suggest that the sacred may be transferred to the Super Bowl? Some have argued so, but fundamentally the answer is no, for the two reasons we have already considered. The Super Bowl is not defined culturally as a place where the sacred should be expressed, and it is not set off from everyday life in a way that would suggest finding the sacred there. It is a special occasion, to be sure, but this is where the defining role of the media becomes a decisive factor. The mere fact that the Super Bowl is televised to the nation means that we associate it culturally with entertainment. Indeed, we can imagine (were it not for the printed news media) that the Super Bowl would have a much more esoteric—perhaps sacred—connotation if we merely heard via the grapevine that it had happened somewhere but did not know exactly what had happened. By the same token, religious services that are televised also take on this connotation. Their removal from sacred congregational space causes something special to be lost. We sense something is wrong, partly because we are able to watch from the (very profane) comforts of our living rooms and partly because the mechanism we are watching is an instrument of entertainment, even though we realize from the words and the pictures that this is not meant to be entertaining.

It is perhaps bizarre to suggest that congregations project the sacred into the public arena without having to say anything specific about God. Were they never to mention God, of course, we would gradually lose the idea that their separateness and the power of the collective gatherings had anything to do with the sacred. But the fact that sacredness inheres in their form, as well as in their content, helps us understand why congregations also cannot get away (at least easily) with making utterances, as it were, *ex cathedra*. Even if a congregation gathers in its sanctuary to discuss business, that business will take on a certain air of sacredness. This is why, incidentally, astute church administrators know it is better to hold business meetings in some other place.

There is, however, one additional way in which the content of what is said in and by congregations is fundamentally important to their capacity to express the sacred. Congregations do not set themselves apart from everyday life simply by hiding out in strange-looking buildings; they do so even more basically by saying strange things and doing strange things. Church services have been likened to carnivals, charivaris, and the festivals of misrule that were common in the Middle Ages. This analogy has not been viewed kindly by churchgoers, yet it holds great truth. In an otherwise secular society the church must in fact be different. It must do strange things to provide a place where the voice of God can at least be imagined, if not actually heard. Clergy do well when they make outrageous statements about love and forgiveness, and congregants do well when they make the even more outrageous attempt to put these statements into practice.

Challenges Facing Congregations

Drawing resources as they do from their host environment, congregations in their efforts to make public the sacred are always subject to changing social conditions. Although some evidence suggests that congregations in the United States may be declining in terms of membership rates, the evidence over the long term seems to indicate continued vitality. Many of the old-line denominations have undergone serious declines in membership, but other denominations and independent congregations have grown dramatically during the same period. The challenges congregations are facing from changing social conditions appear to be more significant in generating qualitative problems for the character of public religion than in endangering the actual survival of most congregations. As always, how particular church leaders respond to these challenges will play a major role in determining the impact they will have.

Because so much of the public religion expressed at the congregation level is the product of clergy efforts, the conditions challenging the authority of clergy roles must be the focus of special attention. Throughout most of the Christian era clergy have been among the leading culture producers in their communities. Only political officials, barristers, patrons of the arts, and men of letters were able to rival the clergy in this regard, and these rivals were generally not as numerous or in as close proximity to the community as the clergy were. As recently as the end of the nineteenth century clergy in the United States were still among the few culture producers in local communities who could command the consistent respect and attention of sizable audiences. All this has of course changed substantially in the twentieth century.

Clergy are now but a small segment of the college-educated, professional, technical, and managerial elite. Even those with three years of training beyond college are likely to be rivaled in most communities by significant numbers of lawyers, doctors, professors, scientists, and engineers with similar levels of education. On most issues of public concern, whether health or the environment, urban problems or interpersonal tensions, other specialists in the community are in a far stronger position to speak with authority than the clergy is. People expect these specialists to make the important decisions. Perhaps more important, vast organizational arrangements have been put in place to ensure that these specialists have a proper role in the production of public culture: universities train them, corporate and government labs pay their salaries, community groups invite them to speak, publishers print their books and articles, news media carry their remarks, and planning boards seek their advice. Clergy may be called in from time to time to bless the proceedings of these meetings or may obtrude as prophets of idealism on more practical matters, but their voice is likely to be restricted primarily to what they can say to their own congregants. The public religion produced by the clergy, therefore, is likely to take the form of reminding the faithful of their higher commitments to absolute values and encouraging them to pray and seek inspiration in their efforts to do right.

This is no inconsiderable contribution to the public sphere, especially when it is the only place in which people hear such admonitions and receive such inspiration. Clergy may not be able to tell their parishioners *how* to stop the arms race, but they can add fervor to the cause by claiming to speak with the reasoned authority of people having God's interests close to heart. The problem of course is that even in this role clergy no longer speak with any special authority. Many parishioners know their pastors spent their seminary years learning little-used esoteric languages and taking courses in counseling and church administration instead of gaining deep knowledge of the Bible or even of life. When clergy admit from the pulpit, as they often seem to do, that they really do not know what the passage means either but are willing to offer some exploratory thoughts, they further undercut their own authority. In a society where people with questions can easily read inspirational books or watch films or attend special seminars, the answers to spiritual questions are perhaps more likely to come from these sources than from the local pastor.

What makes the contribution of the clergy less dismal is that their role consists of much more than proclaiming the voice of the Lord with prophetic authority. They are in fact counselors and administrators, upholding the sacred by keeping individuals and organizations from falling apart. Even in their preaching, their role is probably to remind people of the basic values contained in scripture and tradition or to give a brief time for people to reflect about their lives more than it is to impart an authoritative interpretation. It is, as we have noted, important that the sacred be proclaimed, but the proclamation must also be enacted by the presence and the gathered community of the congregation.

In the Judeo-Christian conception the sacred is always changing while remaining constant in essence, thus introducing a significant sense of history, mission, or journey. Individuals participate in this conception of the sacred by shaping narratives of their own journeys, and congregations sometimes reinforce these narratives by giving individuals opportunities to proclaim them publicly. The congregation provides a crucible in which a new identity, a person undergoing change, can be molded. It also provides a manifestation of the collective journey of the sacred. This is why church leaders know the importance of corporate identity, why congregations write their histories and commemorate their anniversaries, and why they also sometimes deliberately develop conceptions of themselves as mission churches, pilgrim churches, or churches oriented toward new beginnings, rebirth, and revival. These, like our individual stories, are perhaps myths that reconstruct the past and have minimal connections to actual history, yet they play a powerful role in making the sacred concrete. They do so by making it public, visible, so it can be internalized into the consciousness of individual members.

In other contexts these myths have come to be recognized as "organizational culture," and even progressive, profit-oriented business firms know the importance of the narratives making up these myths. In congregations they are perhaps all the more important because of the geographical mobility that affects most churches. Old-timers leave and cannot retell the stories; newcomers do not know them. It thus becomes increasingly valuable for congregations to institute occasions on which their stories can be retold, reenacted, and reconstituted. These occasions may also contribute valuably to the connection that people see between their own congregation and larger public events, such as the opening of the western frontier, the Civil War, the civil rights movement, the assassination of John F. Kennedy, the Vietnam War, efforts to resettle refugees from Southeast Asia, or the AIDS epidemic.

Listening to the narratives people tell about their congregations, though, one cannot help noticing that an overriding theme is often the story of organizational growth and decline. Perhaps it is the pragmatism in our culture, or perhaps it is just that personal and family histories are often associated with it, but the collective memory of

congregations seems to pay inordinate attention to membership figures and the timing of high points and periods of contraction and
expansion. These narratives give a vivid sense of whether people
think their congregations are successful and capable of making a
difference in their communities. Such stories need to be examined
closely. Especially in settings of decline there may be connotations
of remorse and blame, but there can also be hints of closer community, greater wisdom, and deeper caring.

For congregations experiencing decline, their greatest challenge is
likely to be perceived simply as one of survival. Yet the nature of public religion is likely to be deeply influenced by the survival strategies
congregations decide to pursue. Although it is possible for decline
to encourage a sense of futility, many declining congregations have
found needs in their own communities that could still be addressed
effectively with the resources at their disposal. Perhaps the least
recognized challenge, however, is the remedy that many congregations have found in shifting toward a greater array of fee-for-service
programs. Especially when facilities and staff are being underuti-
lized, church leaders may find it attractive to cover the maintenance
costs of these resources by launching a variety of new programs, all
of which are operated on a cash basis: charging rent to twelve-step,
scouting, and other community groups to use the church building;
turning over classrooms during the week to nursery schools that
charge fees sufficient to cover their expenses; offering music lessons
to help defray the costs of having a choir director; putting on concerts for which admission is charged; and so on.

Fee-for-service programs make a good deal of sense as an adaptive
strategy when the broader social environment is increasingly populated with such services. Secular therapists charge hefty fees for their
services, so why should pastors who do counseling be any different?
With more catering services available and more churchwomen who
used to put on church suppers voluntarily now becoming paid members of the labor force, why should not churches charge fees for the
meals they provide? Why should they not pay their choir members
for the time they put in? Why should they not charge fees for classes,
conferences, and retreats, especially when New Age institutes provide spirituality entirely on a fee-for-service basis?

From an economic standpoint it seems only reasonable that congregations will increasingly move in the direction of charging fees

for their services instead of relying on voluntary donations. But the costs to the way in which congregations contribute to public religion must also be considered. We gain a sense of those costs when we look at the impact of shifts from voluntary to fee-for-service arrangements in other sectors: from volunteer fire companies to paid, professional fire departments, from neighborly support to social welfare agencies, and from home cooking to fast-food restaurants. In all three cases market arrangements have moved in to fill a definite need, and in two of the three cases the quality of service overall has probably improved. Yet something has been lost too. It might be described as the personal touch being replaced by impersonality. It might also be described as an erosion of the voluntary spirit itself and with it the moral good that comes from choosing to help out, from acting on principle instead of for pay.

We have long cherished the idea of religious freedom, by which we generally mean the freedom to choose how and whether to worship without fear of government and legal restrictions. We have been less mindful of the ways in which market relations may restrict freedom; indeed, markets are usually associated positively with freedom. It is important, however, to recognize that markets deliver only certain kinds of goods; they do a poor job of providing services for which people cannot pay or even services that only a minority of the public want, especially if that minority cannot pay dearly. We need also to be mindful that freedom implies an act of moral responsibility, whereas market relations imply self-interested calculation. A person who voluntarily engages in some activity is affirming the intrinsic worth of that activity and thus contributing to its reinforcement as a public value, whereas the person who participates in a fee-for-service arrangement demonstrates mainly that the pay received was worth the effort invested. This is why the transactions at fast-food restaurants convey nothing of the caring and nurture of a home-cooked meal. It is also why the paid, professional choir member does not reinforce the value of heart-felt worship in the same way a volunteer does, why buying tickets to attend concerts in a church building is not the same as participating in a worship service itself, and why maintaining church facilities by renting them out to a nursery school dramatizes different values than do meetings people gravitate to because they believe in what is being done. It is why Jesus drove the money changers from the temple.

Apart from these direct consequences for the character of public religion, fee-for-service arrangements are likely to challenge the organizational structure of congregations in such fundamental ways that their ability to articulate public values may be seriously altered. Separate professional, specialized staff members will play an increasing role in directing the futures of congregations, and their interests may well be different from those of the rest of the congregation (who may seldom see these professionals). Congregations will be placed in direct competition with other market-driven professional services, thereby subjecting the church to norms of rational efficiency, and an added premium will be placed on senior clergy who are good bureaucrats instead of spiritual guides. The economic considerations underlying these programs may also make the church subject to the latest fads of a secular society, turn the church into an instrument of the upper middle class that can afford to pay for such services, and foster specialization along new lines that continue to undermine older denominational traditions. The positive consequences may be that these service revenues keep the church from going under entirely, and some people may be drawn into other aspects of the church. The effect on public religion, however, is to squeeze much of the freedom out of its traditional place in the voluntary sector, thus leaving the church relatively indistinct from the doctor's office or the art guild. Still another consequence follows if the congregation becomes involved in services the government pays for; for example, it might distribute meals on wheels voluntarily but get a government subsidy to cover these costs and perhaps even to help cover the rent and administrative overhead. The church then becomes subject to government regulations; this happens even if the services are market oriented, just because the government regulates services involving people, health care, food, and the like. These regulations again may limit the kinds of values a congregation can embody. They can, for example, prevent it from housing the homeless because of its day-care center.

Another challenge facing congregations is the growing pluralism evident in modern societies. American churches have always prided themselves on their pluralism, and the specialization that has developed among congregations in most communities has served them well in adapting to this pluralism. On balance the advantages of pluralism have certainly outweighed the disadvantages. Yet the historic costs need to be recognized, and the prospect of increased pluralism in the future needs to be understood.

The historic costs of pluralism can be measured partly in much duplication of effort. Every congregation has felt the need to provide youth groups, women's auxiliaries, and Sunday school classes for all ages, even when many of these activities barely struggled along for lack of good leadership and sufficient attendance. Recognizing the need for better programs was an important reason for the ecumenical cooperation that began to emerge in local communities during the 1950s and 1960s. Even before that, however, competition among faiths and denominations was causing other functions to be stripped away from religious sponsorship. Municipal hospitals grew not so much because congregations could not collectively provide adequate health facilities but because the divided efforts of Roman Catholics, Presbyterians, and other denominations often resulted in too little of some services and too much of others. During the latter half of the nineteenth century urban elites also increasingly found their common identity not in the churches that divided them but on the museum planning committees and arts councils that united them.

Individual congregations in the past were seldom seriously harmed by these developments because the social niches they occupied were still heavily reinforced by the lines separating neighborhoods, ethnic groups, races, and social classes. When all these lines reinforced one another, the likelihood of church members' having a strong self-identity was increased. Attending church reinforced a set of "deep" values, that is, ones deeply interwoven with what it meant to be a person, a neighbor, and a citizen. The bridges needed to make these values part of one's public responsibilities were already in place.

Increasingly, the social boundaries that define cultural pluralism no longer correspond to the lines around congregations, however, but cut through the middle of these communities. Partly this is because of the megachurch phenomenon that draws people from wider segments of society in the first place to provide more specialized services, and partly it, as well as the megachurch phenomenon itself, is because of geographic mobility, the intermixing of ethnic groups, new bases of social differentiation (such as education), changes in the occupational structure, and the effects of mass consumerism and the mass media. As a result, it is much more likely now than ever before that significant social divisions will exist *within* congregations rather than simply between them. Consequently, there may be less of a sense of actual community, and the congregation itself may splinter into special interest groups.

Prospects and Innovations

The single most likely outcome that will be reinforced by all these challenges—those facing the clergy, the shift to fee-for-service arrangements, and internal congregational pluralism—is an erosion of the ascriptive connotations of public religious values and a heightened emphasis on achievement. Ascription means that religious values are ones felt to be primordial, unalterable, rooted in nature, historic, and inherited characteristics, whereas achievement connotes individual choice, secondary values, and the application of effort and discipline. When clergy base their authority on having received a "call" from God, that is a kind of ascriptive identity; their choice to pursue the call and to spend long years studying and gaining experience is the achieved part of their identity. Congregations that evoke commitment from people just because "this is who we are" are tapping into some ascriptive identity, whereas those that cause people to say "What am I getting out of this?" are linking into a sense of achievement. Ascription and achievement are themselves public values, but they also color public religion with different meanings.

On the positive side the shift from ascription to achievement in congregations means that a greater sense of individual ownership and responsibility is likely to follow. Taking part in something that has "always been done this way" can be a deadening experience compared with doing something because one chooses it. Whatever values a congregation may opt for substantively, whether promoting world peace or cultivating a deeper knowledge of God, these values are likely to generate a greater, more vital commitment from those who have consciously thought them through, chosen freely to become involved with them, and expended enough personal effort that any progress in promoting these values is likely to be considered an achievement. The quality of programs, as well as the level of fervor, is likely to increase when people take the view that they have chosen to do this so they had better do it well.

The negative side is more complicated. Part of the difficulty with an achievement orientation is that much more uncertainty may be entailed in the choice of values itself. Having to think through these choices instead of having them served up in advance can mean that all become relativistic, transient modes of attachment. Part of the difficulty is also that these values are more separated from other segments of one's life. One can choose to work on Tuesday evening for a peace group, much like spending the evening taking tennis lessons, but the traditional relations between one's faith, one's ethnic origins, and one's family were generally more encompassing than this. There is also the danger that meritocratic criteria take the place of all other modes of evaluation. For the clergy it thus becomes better to run a smoothly operating congregation than to head one with a deep sense of mission, or to deliver a sermon eloquently than to give one with substance worth pondering. For the congregants instrumental calculations take precedence, causing questions about effectiveness and personal benefits to outweigh those of intrinsic worth.

It is perhaps symptomatic of these negative implications that the gap between public and private, which we considered earlier, seems to be widening in many congregations, resulting in one of the most significant organizational innovations that the church has witnessed for some time. This is the development of small support groups, both within and outside congregations, in which caring and sharing of personal problems are the dominant concerns. With rising emphasis on instrumental and meritocratic values in the wider programs of congregations, parishioners are likely to feel it necessary to make public only what they do well, to evaluate themselves critically, and yet to put on a happy face indicating that all is well. The deeper, primordial self that used to be rooted in ascriptive identities is likely to be separated from these instrumental, critical, optimistic roles. In response people have found themselves feeling alienated from the very communities of faith in which reconciliation and acceptance are expected to be present. Inauthenticity rather than wholeness has been the subjective counterpart of this alienation. Small groups, shielded from public scrutiny by norms of anonymity, have emerged as efforts to reconstruct a more genuine sense of personal identity. Whether congregations can nurture these groups and whether these groups can lead people back into a more active commitment to public life are questions that remain very much open. Answering these questions is one of the greatest challenges currently facing religious congregations.

3

Hierarchies

I use the term *hierarchies* to refer to religious organizations that operate in an administrative capacity above the level of the congregation to represent these entities and to coordinate their activities. Examples include the organizations generally known as denominational structures and church councils, such as administrative agencies, executive offices, legislative assemblies, church courts, and the various task forces and ad hoc committees that may be formed by these organizations. I reserve treatment of special purpose groups and church colleges and seminaries for subsequent chapters, although these are often related formally and informally to church governing agencies. Through such activities as setting church policies, promulgating confessional and creedal documents, and issuing social statements, religious hierarchies play an important role in shaping public religion.

Dimensions of Variation

Religious hierarchies, like congregations, can be found at every stage in the development of modern Christianity. No sooner had adherents of the new faith begun to establish congregations in the regions of Palestine and Asia Minor than church councils began to appear. Their initial functions included collecting and distributing relief funds to congregations in need, deliberating common teachings, and coordinating missionary and evangelization efforts. As Christianity received official recognition and spread over wider territories, these agencies expanded into vast bureaucracies. By the end of the Middle Ages a central administrative hierarchy was in place in both the western and eastern branches of the church, and a complex pattern of local and regional councils, universities, seminaries, and monastic orders had been established.

While most of these institutions continued and became even more powerful throughout southern and eastern Europe, the Protestant Reformation introduced an alternative set of religious hierarchies in most of the regions of central and northern Europe. In some cases, such as England, the new structures closely resembled the old, often differing only in that different personnel occupied the most important offices and the highest level of authority resided in the king rather than the pope. In other areas, such as the Swiss cantons, religious hierarchies emerged with a much stronger local emphasis than existed in such areas as Denmark, Sweden, and Prussia, where church governance was based on the territorial principle. During the sixteenth and seventeenth centuries the gradual evolution of the absolutist state did much to encourage growth in centralized church councils. At the same time, the religious wars of the period also encouraged a countertendency, involving the formation of smaller, "free," or dissenting religious bodies that emphasized their own autonomy from both the secular state and established religious hierarchies.

This tendency toward religious disestablishment was in full swing when the first American colonies were founded, causing religious bodies to guard jealously against interference in their affairs from the outside. Yet the need for coordination at the supracongregational level was as pronounced in the New World as it was in the Old. Puritans, Anglicans, Catholics, Quakers, and other groups established their own governing agencies to oversee the activities of local congregations, to represent these congregations to their counterpart organizations in Europe, and to coordinate settlement and missionary activities. Denominationalism, with its attendant centralized organizations, was very much a part of American religion from the beginning, particularly because the major religious bodies were transplants of groups that had well-established connections with various territorial regimes and nation-states in Europe. By the time of American Independence these bodies had become stronger on both sides of the Atlantic.

As the new nation spread westward during the nineteenth century, forces arose that worked both for and against the continued growth of religious hierarchies. On the one hand, more churches, larger territory to cover, and a continuing desire to Christianize the indigenous and immigrant populations gave rise to centralized boards and councils oriented toward planning and coordinating these activities. On the other hand, geographic distances, greater heterogeneity of the population, and a political climate of democratization worked to promote congregational autonomy sometimes in active opposition to the centralizing efforts of religious hierarchies.

Much of what we now think of as religious hierarchies is thus a product only of the twentieth century. Although there is strong precedent for many of the current legislative and adjudicatory functions of these organizations, their specific evolution is relatively recent and is indebted to concerted efforts at the end of the nineteenth century to build up more rationally organized administrative bodies. In the twentieth century these efforts continued in fits and spurts, often stimulated by competition between Protestants and Catholics and by competition among Protestant denominations. Over the past half-century additional growth has come about as a result of mergers in many of the mainline Protestant denominations, an interest in these denominations' becoming more truly national in scope and function, growth in the internal activities needing to be supervised, and an effort by religious bodies to respond to the increasingly large-scale problems posed by such secular entities as the modern corporation, government, cities, and the U.S. role in world affairs.

The specific patterns of these hierarchies often reflect long-standing precedents within particular confessional traditions, some vesting greater authority in a centralized administrative office and others providing for greater local autonomy or democratic styles of representation. These patterns nevertheless reflect various combinations of administrative structure that can be understood as variations along several key dimensions or axes that in turn provide insight into some of the historic forces shaping religious hierarchies.

The first of these axes runs along a continuum from centralization to decentralization and reflects centrifugal and centripetal forces of the kind already alluded to in reference to the nineteenth century. Just as in that period, the two continue to work in opposition to each other, both being rooted in institutional and societal considerations.

Forces operating in favor of greater centralization include competition with other centralized bodies, the growing size of organizations in the secular arena, increasing complexity and interdependence of social life in general, and in many traditions some theological precedent for such authority. In favor of greater decentralization are traditions of local congregational autonomy, cost-efficiency concerns, a widespread populist or antibureaucratic sentiment in the general population, and the great diversity of needs and interests in local situations.

A second axis runs along the continuum from an emphasis on a professionalized clergy to an emphasis on lay leadership. This too is an axis along which different traditions can be arrayed and historic movement from one emphasis to the other can be seen. The Reformation is commonly viewed as an assertion of greater lay leadership at the expense of a professionalized clergy, although lay leaders often exercised considerable influence over the late-medieval Catholic church as well. It is important to recognize that religious hierarchies are indeed hierarchies, providing pyramids of power and prestige that professional clergy can ascend. In a secularized society such as our own these hierarchies are likely to be particularly important to clergy because few such opportunities may exist in the wider society. They are likely to be of less interest, except in a negative way, to laity who have ample opportunities to advance in secular hierarchies. There is therefore likely to be (for this as well as for other reasons) an inbuilt tension between clergy and laity. In some hierarchies the clergy has clearly held sway, virtually excluding laity from any significant role in religious hierarchies and setting up highly professional standards of merit and performance for successful clergy to achieve. In other traditions laity have retained greater control for themselves, either by insisting on representation on church boards or by keeping the line between laity and clergy relatively fluid (lay preachers are an example). Clearly the drive toward greater professionalization in the society at large has prompted a similar tendency among clergy that in turn has sometimes precipitated conflict with laity.

Third is an axis rooted in what Max Weber would have referred to as the distinction between rational-legal authority and charismatic authority. Rational-legal authority places strong emphasis on procedural norms, norms of systematization and efficiency, means-ends calculation, and collective deliberation. Charismatic authority vests power primarily in the individual who has a special gift of grace or in related experiences and events that are deemed to be mysterious and beyond rational comprehension. Religious hierarchies have always struggled with the tension between these two kinds of authority, subscribing to the former by virtue of their own bureaucratic form of organization but recognizing the latter as well because of respect for the possibility of divine intervention. At one extreme this tension has been resolved by rational-legal procedural norms that subsume charismatic authority, as in the argument that God's will is inevitably revealed more clearly when men and women of good faith conduct their business according to orderly procedures. At the other extreme charismatic leaders may devise rational-legal structures to carry out their plans but retain the right at any moment to contravene these structures. Clearly there has been great pressure in modern societies for religious hierarchies to adopt rational-legal norms, but it is obvious that charismatic authority is by no means dead.

Finally, a fourth axis that might also be summarized in Weberian terms runs along the continuum from a this-worldly to an other-worldly orientation. This-worldly considerations point toward the importance of everyday life as an arena in which God's purposes can be accomplished; other-worldly orientations diminish the importance of present activities compared with a life to come, such as life after death or a heavenly realm that will be instituted at some point in the future. In religious hierarchies a tension between these two poles is also endemic to a certain extent because hierarchies exist in the real world often for the purpose of acting upon it, yet their very reason for existing is based on a distinction between the sacred and the secular. This tension has resulted in some hierarchies' paying considerable attention to practical affairs, such as the founding of hospitals and orphanages or efforts to influence secular governments. Other hierarchies have been kept to more limited scope because members assumed this world would pass, or else they have grown but largely to foster internal programs, such as education or spiritual retreats.

The Resources for Religious Hierarchies

Although at a practical level religious administrators are probably most affected on a day-to-day basis by the availability or lack of operating funds, we need to remain at the macroscopic level to see in broad terms how religious hierarchies have adapted to the long-range changes that have been taking place in modern societies. The dimensions of variation just considered provide a basis for doing so.

If long-term changes in modern societies have led mainly to a secularization process in which important societal functions have increasingly been divested from religious institutions and placed in secular institutions, then many of the changes that have occurred over the past century or two in religious hierarchies can be understood in these terms. Along each of the four dimensions of variation that we have considered, however, the effects of this secularization process have resulted not in a unitary organizational pattern but in contradictory and opposing tendencies that leave religious hierarchies with room to adapt in a variety of ways, albeit none of which may be entirely satisfactory.

Let us consider, for example, the growth of the bureaucratic nation-state as one of the major developments in modern societies to which religious hierarchies have inevitably been forced to respond. The nation-state is one of the principal resources in the social environment on which religious hierarchies must draw. It is a resource because although it has traditionally struggled against religious hierarchies to attain its own power, it has often given over some of its power to these hierarchies to buttress its own legitimacy. In contemporary societies the nation-state can also be a powerful factor insofar as it sets the legal context in which religious hierarchies must operate, competes with them for citizens' dollars and loyalties, and initiates programs that may harm or benefit the work of religious bodies. The growth of the nation-state is thus of considerable importance.

This growth has in broad terms consisted of two developments: the increasing autonomy of the state from other social institutions and an expansion of the array of social functions for which the state has taken responsibility. Evidence of the former is generally seen in the fact that even the absolutist states of the seventeenth century remained heavily dependent on landlords and merchants to supply revenues and to operate armies, whereas the nation-state of the twentieth century, while hemmed in by complex legal codes, nevertheless exercises far greater coercive powers (potentially at least) over its citizens and operates huge bureaucracies in which professional administrators function with virtual impunity over their own administrative domains. The expansion of state functions is best evidenced by the gradual evolution of social welfare programs since the middle of the nineteenth century and by the greater role most states now play in regulating the economy and guaranteeing favorable conditions in which economic interests can be pursued.

These two developments have had decidedly different implications for the structure of religious hierarchies. At the start of the modern period religious hierarchies in most societies were closely integrated into the activities of the state. In France, for example, prior to the revolution of 1789 the church constituted one of the three primary estates that were represented at all levels of government. In eighteenth-century Scotland the Presbyterian National Assembly was already separate from any of the many British agencies that ruled in Edinburgh, yet members of the assembly continued to exercise great influence over these agencies. In many ways the extreme differentiation of the state, especially from the church, that has been built into the governing framework of the United States has fundamentally weakened religious hierarchies, causing them to function as coordinating bodies for local congregations (such as the Baptist model) rather than as advisers to the king and parliament (as was more the case in Catholic France or Presbyterian Scotland). Yet the expansion of social functions of the state has given religious hierarchies more of a reason to exist than ever before. When welfare functions, for instance, were handled primarily by families and in local communities, congregations themselves were on the front lines of these services, but when social welfare became a matter of centralized government policy, religious bodies could exercise influence only by working through centralized agencies of their own. The joint impact of these changing relations to the state has been that religious hierarchies have been maintained, sometimes even in expanded form, often perpetuating the form and activities that characterized them in an earlier time when they had an official voice in the state. But these hierarchies have had to be maintained voluntarily, through contributions passed along to them by congregations, and have thus had to demonstrate their effectiveness in influencing national policy — or at least in maintaining a "presence" in the nation's capital — to legitimate receiving these voluntary contributions.

The impact of other long-term societal developments has been equally complex for religious hierarchies. If the professionalization of clergy has been encouraged by wider shifts in the occupational structure of modern societies toward professionalization of major segments of the work force, these shifts have also helped undermine the authority of the clergy. In religious hierarchies, just as in congregations, clergy are forced to spend longer years obtaining credentials through formal education and to devote themselves to their work in the same way that professionals pursuing other careers do, yet the result is that clergy are still but one of a growing number of occupations in which similar credentials apply. As in other professions, clergy are encouraged to develop hierarchies as professional associations, among other things, to protect the autonomy of their craft (for example, by restricting entry into theological seminaries). Once created, these hierarchies then become a means in themselves for moving up professional ranks to positions of greater power and responsibility.

Clergy, however, are the only professionals who continue to rely on voluntary donations from their clients. Physicians, dentists, lawyers, therapists, teachers, nurses, and other professionals have been able to use their professional associations, much like trade unions, as a way to set prices for their services and to limit access to their ranks, but clergy remain at the mercy of the laity on whom their financial resources depend. In an otherwise secular society, moreover, the very laity who have greatest control over these financial resources, by dint of their own educational status and professionalism, may have the least respect for the clergy.

Religious hierarchies have, as a result, been both weakened and strengthened by these conflicting tendencies. They have been weakened because lay influence over clergy has generally favored those who provide services at the congregational level, often to the point that local churches have refused to support large centralized programs or, if they did, found laity donating their money to other causes. Religious hierarchies have been strengthened, though, because clergy themselves need these structures more than ever before. Although, unlike other professional associations, they cannot do much to set prices, they do play a major role in restricting access to the profession itself. With limited numbers of pulpits available, this can be a very important role indeed. Moreover, like other professional societies, religious hierarchies can also earn the awe and respect of at least some parishioners by producing esoteric statements couched in specialized jargon, by purporting to represent certain of their interests in high places, and by carrying out activities at a distance and behind closed doors that are assumed to be of importance.

Activities and Audiences

Religious hierarchies in the United States have typically legitimated themselves by engaging in four major activities that could not be carried out by congregations alone: administration, missions, education and publishing, and seminaries. These activities can be found in some form even in the religious hierarchies established by the New Testament church. They became more clearly differentiated in the United States early in the nineteenth century when many missionary societies, publishing houses, Sunday school programs, conference offices, and seminaries were being founded. Even today, as new religious bodies come into being through mergers and schisms, these are the activities on which most attention is centered. Not only do these activities provide a continuing rationale for religious hierarchies but their changing content and composition constitute the principal means by which religious hierarchies contribute to the public expression of the sacred.

It is obvious enough that the mission programs of the churches have historically been one of the major ways in which the sacred was made public and that these programs could not have existed on such a large scale without the careful coordination of religious hierarchies. Over the past half-century or so many old-line denominations have adopted such universalistic theological orientations that the rationale for their mission programs has become virtually anachronistic, and as a result these programs have either declined precipitously or have changed radically in purpose. In terms of overt missionary activities, Evangelical and sectarian religious bodies, such as Assemblies of God and Mormons, have thus come to be the major public influence in the United States and in many other parts of the world. The enormous attention given in old-line Protestant and Catholic religious hierarchies to the poor through welfare and relief efforts can be seen partly as a replacement for the earlier missionary activities of these hierarchies.

Religious education, publishing, and the training of clergy continue to be important functions of religious hierarchies as well, but in all these areas the virtual monopoly that religious hierarchies once held has been broken. Sunday school teachers in most religious bodies can, for example, obtain materials from independent distributors and use it at will instead of having to follow prescribed curriculums. Publishing houses may still specialize in books about a certain denomination or by authors from that tradition, but they are likely to carry diverse listings as well. Seminary training may be received at independent institutions rather than from those sponsored by particular denominations.

Although these traditional functions continue, the role of religious hierarchies in promulgating and shaping public religion may be even more important in other areas. As already suggested, the way in which these hierarchies function as professional societies for clergy may have an increasingly significant impact, if indirect, on public religion insofar as clergy opinions and activities are shaped by these societies. In an era of continuing disputes over theological, moral, and social issues, religious hierarchies are also likely to play an important role in arbitrating these disputes. How a church court or assembly settles certain cases can have a major impact on whether laity continue to support the church's programs or whether, in the extreme, they disaffiliate or form splinter groups. Insofar as media and other secular institutions look to religious bodies for guidance, religious hierarchies are also likely to be the source to which they turn, if only because centralized, certified agencies are increasingly the social norm in all areas of public life.

Although on paper it may appear that religious hierarchies are well-organized agencies structured along lines of functional responsibility to further the cause of making the sacred public in several strategic areas, the reality is likely to be quite different. Religious hierarchies are particularly likely to be the focus of controversy, conflict, and internal division, not only because they have an adjudicatory role but also because they, like most bureaucracies, combine overlapping and contradictory ladders of ascent and constituencies. In addition to all the tensions already mentioned, religious hierarchies are likely to be torn by serving in various capacities all of the following constituencies: laity within congregations, clergy within congregations, clergy and laity working in such noncongregational ministries as foreign missions or schools, full-time paid staff of the central agencies themselves, and the wider public.

The ladders of ascent by which clergy move into religious hierarchies are also likely to ensure a high degree of internal tension. In most Protestant denominations, for example, a common means of ascent is by working up from smaller congregations to larger congregations, all the while playing an active role in regional conferences, presbyteries, synods, or associations, and thus winning elective office by virtue of grass-roots popularity and support. An equally common route into the hierarchy, however, is by isolating oneself from congregational influences and taking appointive offices within the bureaucracy itself or in other noncongregational settings, such as seminaries. The former ladder is likely to elevate clergy with more conservative theological and moral inclinations that mirror those of their constituents at the grass roots. The latter is likely to elevate clergy with more liberal theological and moral inclinations that reflect their insulation from the grass roots and their advocacy or intellectual roles in specialized agencies. In Roman Catholic settings similar divisions may be evident between parish priests, on the one hand, and clergy in orders, academic settings, and specialized ministries, on the other. Such divisions have, in fact, been crucial to the shaping of public religion on numerous occasions over the past half-millennium.

Expressing Public Religion

Religious hierarchies, by their nature, seldom produce anything that evokes deep-felt wonder or a sense of being in subjective contact with the sacred. Their contribution to public religion is much more likely to occur in discursive and rational form. After all, they include deliberative agencies whose job is to resolve disputes and determine policy goals and perspectives to guide the activities of a larger number of congregations. These directives must be framed in sufficiently general and abstract language that they can be applied to congregations in a wide variety of settings; often their public includes political leaders and readers of the national media who are not members of these congregations.

Because they do not initiate liturgies or provide supportive communities, we might suppose that religious hierarchies contributed little to the public expression of the sacred. Yet these hierarchies probably produce more of what is commonly regarded as public religion than does any other source. This is because the position papers and policy statements produced by religious hierarchies have continued to be taken as important contributions to shaping public religion. Such statements have, of course, been issued by religious bodies virtually since the beginning of Christendom. Indeed, Christendom itself owes its existence to the various councils that took place early in its history to hammer out positions on controversial issues and to establish creeds. In each subsequent period of the church's development similar councils met to decide the burning issues of the time. These councils were often, in turn, deeply influenced by the powerful political and economic elites whose interests were at stake, but to say this is to take nothing away from the councils themselves. Well into the modern period, religious assemblies continued to issue statements that sovereigns were expected to implement, and dissenters from these statements could find themselves living outside the law and their very lives in danger.

The higher assemblies of many of the old-line faiths, such as the Roman Catholic, Presbyterian, Episcopal, and Lutheran churches, continue to issue periodic pronouncements on matters of social and political importance, and these statements are still put forth in tones that suggest their authors may have the ghosts of John Knox or Thomas Cranmer looking over their shoulders. Position papers on peace, nuclear arms, racial discrimination, and sexuality are made public at regular intervals by these higher assemblies with the ostensible purpose of influencing the public arena directly. The news media are expected to give these papers wide coverage, and religious leaders hope in the process to influence not only their own adherents but also the public officials who set the direction of national policy.

Paying close attention to the language of these statements and to those responsible for them generally indicates that more modest aims are shared as a kind of fallback position. If, for example, it is denied that a statement about homosexuality actually indicates official church doctrine on this subject, it is nevertheless hoped that the statement will be used as a teaching tool and that it will promote discussion. Or if religious leaders do not expect public officials to borrow directly from the language of a statement about human rights, they at least hope such a statement will help galvanize the courage of those who are lobbying on behalf of this cause. It is not often clear, however, what role these statements actually play in contemporary settings where neither the church nor those exercising sovereignty in secular affairs seem compelled to regard them as enforceable truth.

In the most favorable light the policy statements issued by high religious assemblies conform to the most desirable aspects that are usually associated with an ideal public sphere. They are the result of collective deliberations in which all relevant parties are invited to participate regardless of their positions and the views of all parties are considered; moreover, standard conventions of public debate and rational argument are employed in these deliberations, and the products are framed in rational language, widely disseminated, and allowed to succeed or fail on the basis of persuasion alone rather than coercion. Indeed, it has often been pointed out that secular democratic traditions of government owe much to the legacy of religious assemblies in which deliberations following these patterns were the accepted norm.

Given the possibility of viewing the statements of religious assemblies in such a favorable light as this, why is the actual response typically far more negative? We can understand why in particular cases because there are always dissenting voices who register their substantive disagreements by attempting to discredit the entire process. There is often more involved than this, however. At least three reasons can be given for the widespread negative reaction that seems so often to be aroused by such statements. One is that in a secular society where policies are chiefly in the hands of specialized political bodies such statements seem futile and thus evoke grumbling even among those who might agree with them. This response is much like that of people who view the debates televised from the House of Representatives and Senate with cynicism because they believe the real power lies elsewhere, perhaps with the executive branch. When religious assemblies issue statements, the resulting cynicism is likely to be multiplied by the fact that political leaders do not listen and the authority of religious leaders even to speak is often questioned. A second reason for negative reactions is that people on the religious or political right are likely to see the whole process as a form of tampering with sacred traditions. How, they would argue, can any human assembly presume to know better than what has already been discerned traditionally from holy writ? Their response is like that of the true believers in positivist science, of whom there are still many, who would see the debates of a scientific committee as a silly exercise because either something is already true or it is not. The third reason for negative reactions, probably associated more often with religious or political liberals, is that any group presuming to speak with divine authority is viewed skeptically in relation to prevailing secular norms of individual relativism and tolerance. This reaction is like that of people who chafe at the laws of their community, saying to themselves, "What right do those people have to tell me how to live my life?" In the religious sphere this response is likely to be especially strong, even when such statements are not binding, because religious conviction is so often viewed as a matter of individual conscience alone.

With these cultural orientations already predisposing people to respond negatively, it is all the more puzzling that public religious statements continue to be issued in the manner they are. Even when they are put forth as nonbinding resolutions, they are often buttressed by the institutional authority of the church: by being presented on behalf of the entire denomination or faith; by being advanced from "on high," that is, by an element of the religious hierarchy; and in many cases by carrying the added weight of a requirement that they be disseminated to, and perhaps even voted on by, constituents in the congregations. The news media aggravate the problem by failing to indicate the exact nature of authorship and intent, but religious hierarchies themselves contribute to the problem by shielding the names of individual authors and disseminating statements simply in the name of the church.

The possibility of doing things differently can be recognized by considering the alternative that is more frequently used in academic and scientific circles. Suppose some issue of national concern that also has a strong scientific or technological component, such as questions of global warming or the issue of how best to dispose of toxic waste, is to be discussed. Instead of the government's issuing a statement under the name of the government itself, an independent body, such as the National Academy of Sciences, would likely be asked to form a study group. Scholars with credentials among their peers and from different fields and perspectives would be assembled, and their report would be issued as a summary of what the group could say consensually, but there would perhaps be a minority statement as well. Such a report never succeeds in satisfying all critics, especially those who see the entire process as futile or think the answer must await definitive research; nevertheless, it does contribute understanding on matters of pressing public concern.

This is perhaps the model that religious assemblies have in mind when they commission scholars to study timely issues from a theological perspective. Such commissions can contribute understanding beyond that of the work of individual theologians or ethicists, just as scientific commissions can augment the research of their separate members. Yet religious assemblies generally insist on going further. Rather than let the study be conducted under the auspices of an independent body (perhaps some professional religious studies association), they retain control over the process, keeping it within the church hierarchy. They then attempt to add weight to the work of the authorities who wrote the statement by voting on it in some larger assembly. Such a vote should of course contribute to wider public debate and reflection, but in practice it often seems to encourage polarization and the use of acrimonious language.

The thrust of these considerations is to suggest that religious hierarchies contribute to the public arena not only through the content of their resolutions and position papers but also by the manner in which these statements are made. It may seem more risky to unloose statements from their moorings in an area of broad values than on a narrow scientific topic, but societies seeking so desperately to find answers to troubling evaluative questions would certainly still pay attention to such statements. Their authority, it appears, would also be enhanced by associating them with the work of bodies of individuals known for their expertise on particular subjects more than with the mere authority of bureaucratic position and process. These statements would perhaps then be more numerous and more diverse, but they would continue to guide public deliberations and provide checkpoints against which to compare the counsels of individual conscience.

Organizations and Types of Expression

Policy statements are only one of the cultural products of religious hierarchies. If it is possible to think of uncoupling these statements from the hierarchical structure of religious organizations themselves, it is less conceivable to sever the links between these organizations and other fruits of their labors. Where they are essential is in deciding on the actual character and distribution of resources to collective activities of the church itself. Money for foreign missions provides the classic example. Because it made no sense for separate congregations to sponsor ill-conceived or overlapping mission programs, these programs came to be centralized under the authority of religious hierarchies. How much money to allocate to this purpose, what the credentials of missionaries should be, and whether to direct it mainly to one continent or another were questions that required some means of arriving at collective agreement. Other matters that necessitated the same process included the founding of seminaries and colleges, the determination of official policy on certain doctrines and liturgical practices, and rules governing such corporate roles as officers, representatives, and membership. Some of these could be decided by agreeing to let lower agencies, such as regional assemblies or congregations, have the final word, thus institutionalizing an agreement to disagree.

If we refer to these kinds of issues as questions of resource allocation, we can see there is a decided difference between such issues and the policy statements with which we were concerned in the previous section. Whereas resource allocation questions concern the distribution and control of scarce goods belonging to members of the organization itself, policy statements focus on matters of importance to the wider society. Both are relevant considerations for public religion, but the impact of the former is likely to be indirect, while the influence of the latter is at least intended to be direct. The chief problem is that some resolutions incorporate both concerns, thereby causing confusion by virtue of the organizational means used to ratify the two. Resource allocation questions clearly need to be made in a way that is binding on the entire organization, but policy statements can be issued that are primarily informational and can serve that purpose for nonmembers as well as members. A resolution about, say, the ordination of women falls into the former category, but this resolution may also contain arguments about gender equality that fit more nearly into the latter. Handling the two through different organizational procedures would probably be in the best interest of both.

Looking at these two kinds of issues over time would suggest there has probably been an increase in both but perhaps a more recent and steeper rate of ascent in policy statements. Resource allocation questions became more acute in the earlier part of the twentieth century as religious hierarchies took on more functions and attempted to do so on a societywide scale. In recent years efforts to decentralize some of these functions by returning them to congregational auspices has perhaps reduced the importance of resource allocation issues, although scarcity has perhaps outweighed some of this reduction by making it all the more important for these resources to be allocated judiciously. Policy statements, in contrast, can be issued with less attention to organizational resources themselves, and religious bodies appear to have become increasingly convinced about the importance of such statements because political institutions and the media have created a more distinct sense of a single national culture. Perhaps unsurprisingly, those religious bodies in which overall resources have been declining thus appear to be "talking" more at the same time they are "doing" less.

It might be supposed that the considerable historical disputes separating the various styles of church government from one another would still be evident in the manner in which the various bodies produce and disseminate policy statements. This is to some extent the case. For example, religious bodies governed by groups of bishops often seem to be able to issue statements with little evidence of internal dissension within the issuing body itself, whereas those with congregationally representative styles of governance are less able to hide such dissension. The more dominant feature, however, appears to be an isomorphic tendency across all organizational styles. Let some issue emerge in the wider culture, and within a few years every major religious body will have issued a statement about it.

Prospects and Innovations

It is as inconceivable in the religious sphere to think that religious hierarchies will fade from existence as it is in the economic sphere to envision the demise of the corporation. Both play a vital role in co-ordinating the activities of the smaller units in which production—of the sacred or of material goods—takes place. But, just as in the corporate sphere, religious hierarchies will be in continuous flux, adapting to changes necessitated by their own internal processes, new technologies, government regulations, and consumer demands.

For several reasons it seems likely that religious hierarchies will focus more of their attention on issues at the national level. Through a series of mergers most of the larger hierarchies now represent constituent churches that are scattered throughout the nation and feel entitled to discuss issues widely applicable to their constituents. Since resistance to particular issues is usually rooted in localized concerns, religious bodies are also increasingly likely to take the route followed in political affairs, using the federal level to overcome this resistance. Clergy who feel unable to work for peace and justice because of strong military interests in their districts are thus likely to look to national assemblies and central agencies to counterbalance these interests. The analogy with the federal government also suggests that religious hierarchies will feel themselves especially responsible for providing the same high-level public witnesses that the government does. For example, opposition to a presidentially initiated war in some corner of the world will be considered more effective if it comes from an agency representing all Episcopalians, Methodists, or Catholics than if it comes only from a special interest group. Finally, the professionalization of clergy in an age of rapid communication also makes it increasingly likely that clergy will feel the importance of having national agencies to represent their legal and economic interests and to manage their public image in the mass media.

One of the most likely innovations, indeed one that is already taking place, in religious hierarchies may consist of changing relations between clergy and their clients. An increasing emphasis on fee-for-service relations will have far-reaching effects at this level, just as it will in congregations. Especially in communions with declining membership and fewer clergy positions, the balance of clergy employment will shift toward involvement in other ministries, such as counseling services and clinics, chaplaincy programs in hospitals, teaching, and government work. As ordained clergy, the individuals employed in these settings will presumably still be eligible for service on a part- or full-time basis on church committees, boards, and agencies. Their interests, however, are likely to be quite different from those of clergy in traditional parish roles. Sermon preparation and the attendant attention to Bible study and theological interpretation may play little or no part in these fee-for-service or salaried settings. People with special needs, such as the physically challenged or homeless, may be of much greater immediate interest than they are in the traditional (suburban) congregational setting. Clergy may also be in secular organizations dealing with specific policy questions or advocacy initiatives.

Both the content and the channels of public religion may therefore become radically different. In the past the missionary, educational, and adjudicatory functions of religious hierarchies have operated chiefly on the same principle as that of the local congregation, except on a larger scale or with a different audience in mind. Preaching, teaching, and discussing biblical concepts were the primary means of communication. Indeed, the sermon is still very much the model followed, even when religious bodies issue social statements whose audience is presumably more diffuse. The language and format are understandable to those within the subculture of these bodies, but they often are not easily conveyed by other media. Newspapers and television, for example, are generally not in the habit of printing sermon texts, instead preferring reportage of "events," such as a shooting, a fire, or at least a speech. What may be reported about a social statement, then, may be not the statement itself but a vignette of some angry preacher lambasting it or some newscaster making "commentary" about it. The newer roles and constituencies represented in religious hierarchies are more likely to be effective by eliminating the sermon model entirely. Public religion will in their view be better advanced, as is already sometimes seen, through stockholder initiatives, behind-the-scenes lobbying, and the work of secular organizations themselves.

If religious hierarchies become more bureaucratic in their own right and more influential in working through other bureaucratic means, there is the danger they will succeed in killing the spirit that has always made the sacred what it is. Debate still occurs but behind closed doors, and it inevitably excludes everyone without the power to gain access to these conference rooms and corridors. It may be public in the sense of affecting the wider society, but it is no longer as public in the sense of being open to collective scrutiny and participation. To guard against this danger, some religious agencies have consciously chosen to identify themselves as "anti-structures," as places where the poor and oppressed especially are welcomed. The work of these agencies also needs to be done with space allocated for the mysterious qualities of the sacred itself to be preserved.

Ironically, preserving the sacred may run contrary to the very purpose of religious hierarchies. They are, after all, social control mechanisms. Their purpose, among others, is to maintain order so that religion is not embarrassed in public life. They may not discipline heretics as they did in the Middle Ages, but they accomplish the same purpose by defining heresy out of existence, embracing the widest possible range of interpretations and life-styles, making them so acceptable that scandal cannot occur. Some scandal may be necessary, however, for the sacred to have a genuine role in public life. It may be that the sacred itself, at some fundamental level, is scandalous.

4

Special Interests

Although congregations and religious hierarchies exhaust the organizational forms that have traditionally been associated with the production of public religion, special interest groups have in recent decades greatly augmented the ways in which these established organizations function. Special interest groups generally take shape around a single issue, such as lobbying for legislation that would allow prayer in public schools or representing the special needs of a religious minority group, and their activities are geared to accomplish a relatively specific goal or set of goals. Some special interest groups have successfully developed organizations that span the entire nation and channel resources to central agencies attempting to influence federal policies, while many more special interest groups operate informally and at the local community or regional level.

Religious special interest groups are particularly important to consider in any effort to understand the ways in which public religion is created and expressed because these groups are often concerned with setting and shaping the national agenda concerning fundamental questions of morality and social ethics. Much of the activity of congregations is devoted to the private spirituality of individual parishioners, and denominational hierarchies are often concerned with administrative matters that primarily affect their own constituencies. In contrast, special interest groups have increasingly been launched as a means of influencing public discourse directly, and these groups typically address what have been called "public goods," or issues that affect an entire society. These groups generally operate in opposition to one another, functioning as "struggle groups" whose aim is to win some objective against the resistance of other groups with opposing objectives.

These groups can be found on a limited basis in historical settings at least as far back as the early part of the nineteenth century, but their character and social role has changed dramatically in the past quarter-century alone. They appear to be one of the important ways in which religion is adapting to changing social and cultural circumstances. Understanding how they function is thus a way to see more broadly how the challenges of contemporary society are influencing the shape and content of the sacred.

The Varieties of Special Interest Groups

Because they tend to focus on single issues, special interest groups can readily be classified according to the various categories of issues with which they are concerned. Some of the main issues that have been the basis for religious special interest groups include foreign missionary work, evangelization, educational activities, relief ministries, youth ministries, representation of the professional needs of clergy, minority groups, peace and justice, and public affairs. A comparison of these issues with the functions of religious hierarchies discussed in the last chapter reveals a high degree of similarity. Special interest groups have in fact arisen frequently under the sponsorship of denominational hierarchies or to supplement the work of these agencies. Some of the first special interest groups, for example, emerged to streamline and prevent duplication of efforts by denominational mission boards and Bible societies. The long-term trend, however, has been for special interest groups to disaffiliate from sponsoring denominations and for an increasing number to be initiated independently from such hierarchies. A secondary mode of classification, therefore, is whether the group is still in some way connected with a denominational hierarchy or is genuinely autonomous.

The great variety of contemporary religious special interest groups can partly be explained on the basis of their denominational origins. Because the United States is a religiously pluralistic country, special interest groups are more numerous and varied. During the 1960s, for example, several mainstream Protestant denominations initiated black caucuses to carry out some of the concerns that had been emphasized by the civil rights movements. Soon there were black caucuses in other mainstream Protestant denominations, in the Catholic church, and in many of the smaller sects as well. Each was a religious special interest group representing a particular segment of the larger religious population. With such diversity stemming from denominational origins, special interest groups have also proliferated because other constituents felt the need for an independent, nondenominational group, and still other groups have been founded to coordinate the efforts of several denominational constituencies.

Diversity among special interest groups also exists because modern religion has generally tried to make itself relevant to the society in which it exists. As different issues have arisen, religious leaders have tried to address them instead of arguing that such issues are just passing fads or should be left to secular agencies. In the early nineteenth century, for example, religious leaders founded special interest groups to meet the challenges of a growing population, westward expansion, service to indigenous peoples, and participation in the nation's growing role, along with European societies, in colonizing remote lands. Many of the groups founded during this period are still active or have spawned successor groups that are active in missionary, Bible distribution, translation, and relief efforts. By the end of the nineteenth century the new challenges posed by industrialization and an expanding immigrant population in the cities had led to the founding of another kind of special interest group. Today such organizations as the Young Men's Christian Association (YMCA), the Woman's Christian Temperance Union (WCTU), and the Salvation Army bear witness to the efforts initiated during that period. In the twentieth century each decade or two has generated another set of issues that has prompted additional special interest groups. Women's, children's, and youth organizations came into being, for example, between the 1930s and 1950s, when the nuclear, suburban family was in the forefront of national concern. In the 1960s civil rights groups and antiwar groups proliferated. More recent developments have included feminist organizations, pro- and anti-abortion groups, associations representing the interests of homosexuals, and lobbying groups concerned with these and other issues, such as the interests of veterans and the needs of the physically challenged.

To a significant degree special interest groups contain an internal "multiplier" that adds to their number and variety as well. Because they are concerned with public policy and with making claims on public goods, they tend to develop on both sides of every issue. Any sudden round of special interest groups concerned with lobbying, say, for easing laws against euthanasia would immediately elicit another wave of such groups aimed at countering the efforts of the first. The representative nature of these groups also adds to their number and variety. Were a pro-euthanasia bill to be initiated, it would not be sufficient for a single religious interest group to emerge in support of this bill; to show how strong (and wide) the support was, it would be important for there to be a Catholic pro-euthanasia group, groups from all the major Protestant denominations, and probably "second-level" groups built on top of other interest groups as well, such as an evangelical feminists' pro-euthanasia group, a gay Mormon pro-euthanasia group, and so on.

Because special interest groups represent particular issues and particular constituencies, then, their diversity is likely to be extremely high. Representing a narrow space in the public arena, as it were, there is simply much more space left for other groups to occupy. Their chances of multiplying are much greater than are those of multipurpose organizations. Congregations, for example, are likely to be interested in a wide variety of issues facing their parishioners and their communities at any given time. When these issues change, they may reallocate some of their resources (say, by starting a new committee and disbanding an old one), but their standing functions can also incorporate these changes without major organizational realignment by, for example, considering them as part of Sunday school classes, in sermons, or at meetings of vestries or deacon boards. In contrast the very reason for the existence of special interest groups — often stated clearly in their incorporating charter and bylaws — is to address a delimited goal. Their officers will do their best to continue pursuing this goal, even if new issues arise. When such issues do arise, a new group is likely to come into being.

Constituents and Resources

It has been common to view religious special interest groups as extensions of the churches, helping these established organizations to meet new needs or to play a more effective role in the wider society.

The term *parachurch organization* has often been used to capture this sense of a specialized ministry—a group that extended beyond the religious community itself and did not attempt to provide all the functions of a church but did augment the work of the church by bringing specialized talents to bear in a particular area, such as evangelization, youth programs, educational publishing, lobbying, or public relations. Because of this complementary role, religious leaders have generally understood the rise of special interest groups as a product of two factors: large needs that the churches themselves were unable to fill and a willingness on the part of the churches to share some of their resources to help meet these needs.

Both of these factors are important. The need to provide food and other kinds of physical assistance to people in underdeveloped parts of the world, for example, is a reason for the existence of religiously sponsored relief agencies, and the donations of churches are a key factor in the ability of these agencies to carry out their mission. In this perspective the strength of congregations and religious hierarchies is a principal reason for the existence of so many special interest groups. There is much truth in this argument. Certainly the United States, with strong religious institutions of other kinds, has been able to mount greater efforts in the area of specialized ministries than have societies with weaker religious institutions. Yet this argument illumines only a small part of the larger picture.

Religious special interest groups need to be understood in relation to the wider environmental resources and constituencies that make them possible in the first place and that influence their contribution to the public expression of religious values. Among these conditions it is especially important to consider the relationship between religious special interest groups and the secular emphasis of contemporary society, the growing role of the state, and the highly rationalized character of modern institutions.

The secular emphasis of contemporary society suggests an argument that runs directly counter to the view that religious special interest groups flourish essentially because other religious institutions are strong. To understand how secularity has contributed to the rise of special interest groups, let us consider a hypothetical society in which nothing ranked nearly as high on the scale of absolute values as debates over fine points of theological interpretation. In such a society—were there freedom to do so—new religious organizations would most likely emerge when some group of people became convinced that its theological interpretation was right and all others were wrong. Doctrinal issues that affected the way in which people worshiped the divine would be especially generative of such organizational initiatives. For example, a group that believed the Eucharist should be celebrated as a token of Christ's body and blood might well differentiate itself from another group that believed this sacrament really was the body and blood, rather than merely a token, and from yet another group that deprived it of any special status at all.

Such debates were in fact the kind of controversies that gave rise to new religious organizations during the Protestant Reformation in the sixteenth century. Geographic and political factors played a role as well, but the reasons used to justify new organizations were framed in fundamental theological language. Contemporary special interest groups founded by religious leaders take a quite different form. They respond to the challenges presented by secular considerations, such as how can we curb the proliferation of nuclear weapons, or how can Congress be persuaded to restrict abortions? This is not to say that religious communities should not be concerned with such issues or that they should return to recondite arguments about transubstantiation. Even to suggest that religious communities focus on theological issues rather than the pressing concerns of the day seems awkward because of the very strong orientation toward the secular that prevails in contemporary societies. Religious special interest groups may reflect the strength of established religious institutions, but they also show that these institutions are fundamentally oriented toward the secular world. The proliferation of such groups in recent years is thus evidence that religious organizations feel compelled to be active participants in the world in which they live. This orientation is simply a precondition, a cultural assumption, on which the possibility of special interest groups' existing at all depends.

The growing role of the state in contemporary society has contributed most to shaping the *content* of religious special interest groups. Over the long haul this influence is very easy to discern. The missionary and Bible societies of the early nineteenth century may have been shaped in a remote way by government policies that made it possible for white settlers to move into new territories or for trading vessels to ply the waters of distant continents, but fundamentally these special interest groups were launched to extend the kind of

ministries that were already available in established churches. At the
end of the twentieth century the role of government is much more
evident. Religious special interest groups proliferate to lobby Capitol Hill for various bills that have moral implications or affect the
ability of religious organizations to carry on their basic ministries.
Even with shorter-term comparisons, the rising influence of the state
can sometimes be clearly recognized. As recently as the 1960s, for
example, conferences to which religious leaders were invited generally were structured primarily to reflect the religious pluralism
and the growing mood of ecumenism of the day—token representation of Catholics, Jews, and the major Protestant denominations. By
the 1980s similar conferences were more likely to be dominated by
representatives of Washington-based organizations and to focus on
achieving a balance of politically conservative and politically liberal
groups (or of representing one to the exclusion of the other).

The growing role of the state is generally manifested in public
monies amounting to a greater share of the overall national bud-
get; employment in the government sector rising as a proportion of
the total labor force; greater centralization of governmental functions either through an actual shift of responsibility from state and
local units to federal agencies or through greater coordination by the
federal government of lower units; greater regulation of the private
sector by government; more activist intervention by government
agencies in fiscal and economic matters; and an enormous increase
in the use of the courts for settling all kinds of domestic disputes. In
the United States the political sector remains highly fragmented and
only loosely coordinated compared with the bureaucratic governing
institutions that exist in many European countries and in Japan, yet
the political sector plays a much more active and encompassing role
in the wider society than it did even a few decades ago.

The effects of this growth in the political sector on religious
special interest groups have been both direct and indirect. Direct
effects have included challenges to established religious organizations by legislative actions, the courts, and executive-branch agencies
that have in turn prompted special interest groups concerned with
contesting these challenges and lobbying for more favorable consideration. Such actions have included court rulings against prayer
in public schools, Federal Communication Commission investiga-
tions of religious television programming, and Internal Revenue Ser-

vice cases against parochial schools. Direct effects have not always been negative, however. Numerous entitlement programs have been launched by the federal government that have made it possible for religious special interest groups, such as charities, shelters, orphanages, and food distribution programs, to receive subsidies from public funds. Indirect effects of government expansion have been extremely varied, ranging from playing a stronger role in the setting of public agendas (especially through the political use of the mass media), to creating a more unified national culture, to defining new subnational constituencies through entitlement programs and equal opportunity legislation. By setting the public agenda, political leaders have forced religious groups to respond to these issues if they are to have any say at all in public affairs. In defining a more unified national culture — for example, through public schools and uniform legislation — government has encouraged religious special interest groups to develop at the national level as well. The various entitlement programs have clearly played a role in encouraging the growth of religious groups oriented to such constituencies as African Americans, senior citizens, and the physically challenged.

The highly rationalized character of modern institutions has been a critical influence on the *form* of religious special interest groups — an effect that has also helped shape their content. What this means is that religious special interest groups exist in an environment dominated by other formal organizations, including business firms, nonprofit organizations, and government bureaus, and by a highly complex system of legal rules and regulations. Religious special interest groups are consequently constrained to follow carefully prescribed procedures of incorporation and operations and to adopt familiar organizational styles. For example, these groups are generally incorporated under the tax laws and state codes governing tax-exempt public charities or private foundations, and this mode of incorporation requires them to have a director, a board of trustees, a written statement of mission that clearly delineates their activities, a set of bylaws, regular meetings, and approved and audited budgets. These same rules prevent them from engaging in lobbying activities or, if they do so, require them to report political contributions and prevent them from filing for tax exemption. Many of these rules are clearly stated by the legal statutes governing nonprofit organizations. How these rules are interpreted and implemented, however, depends greatly on the informal, but quite real, presence of other rationalized organizations in the immediate contexts in which religious special interest groups function. Attorneys that provide legal counsel for these groups, for instance, are likely to have experience in dealing with other nonprofit and for-profit organizations. Boards of trustees are likely to be chosen to include persons with experience in business, government, and nonprofit administration. Directors will probably seek advice from their counterparts in other organizations.

All this means that religious special interest groups are likely to function as formal organizations rather than as informal communities of individuals who happen to be interested in the same issues. The activities of these organizations will take recognizable and fairly predictable form. The fact that they do, moreover, constrains the ways in which they pursue their various objectives. A lone individual concerned about the number of abortions taking place, for example, might stand on the corner and yell obscenities at passing motorists (or build homemade bombs to throw into the offices of family planning clinics), but special interest groups concerned about the same issue would seldom deviate from a prescribed package of activities, such as holding public lectures, debating procedures at annual trustees' meetings, or employing an attorney to bring suit against local clinics.

The relationship between religious special interest groups and their environment is thus a symbiotic one. For their part, these groups are able to flourish because the broader environment is already heavily laden with such groups. They can draw on the professional expertise of the other organizations, use tested fund-raising tactics, purchase operating manuals, and follow rules of the game that are well institutionalized. Their capacity to function would be severely limited if they had to develop all these resources from scratch (as missionaries in underdeveloped countries often discover). But the rationalized and formally organized character of the social environment, in turn, is reinforced by the fact that religious special interest groups conform so closely to its procedures. These groups may bring religious values to the attention of public officials, or they may bring public issues to the attention of their faith constituencies. By doing so, they may indeed help steer abortion policy in one direction or another or influence the way public monies are allocated to the poor. Yet they also contribute to an underlying cultural consensus that values formality, rationality, legality, and even government as dearly as life itself.

How the Sacred Is Produced

It follows from what we have just observed that special interest groups, even those appealing primarily to religious constituencies, are in one sense not principally designed to produce the sacred at all. Unlike congregations, for example, they are generally not concerned with providing liturgical contexts in which the sacred can be experienced directly or theological instruction aimed at communicating a broad understanding of the nature of God. Special interest groups, it might be said, are more concerned with the ethical consequences that derive from certain understandings of the sacred than with these understandings themselves. Their role is to identify certain practical applications or courses of action that can be justified in moral terms and to pursue ways of translating these agendas into concrete programs.

Recognizing their practical orientation, special interest group leaders have often differentiated sharply between moral aims and sacred principles. In certain cases they may do so by arguing that their moral agendas are ones on which people of decency can agree no matter what their particular view of the divine may be. In other cases they may argue that the programs they are championing have a certain urgency or compelling force but are more subject to human interpretation than are basic truths about the sacred. In either case the moral aims are rendered more adaptable to their social circumstances than if they were linked more closely to conceptions of the divine. Where morality is said to be more universal than particular interpretations of the divine are, moral behavior can be advanced without becoming embroiled in theological controversies. Where morality is said to be more relativistic, it can be associated with programs that vary from place to place or that can be modified when circumstances change. If conservative special interest groups have tended to argue for the universalism of their moral claims and liberal groups for relativistic applications, it should be noted that both kinds of groups benefit from this separation of the moral from the sacred.

The line between morality and the sacred is, however, seldom

drawn in absolute terms. A program to outlaw the killing of un-
born infants may be presented in terms of common human decency, but it will also likely refer at some point to conceptions of
the soul or to divinely inspired definitions of what it means to be
human. Were the moral injunction to be separated completely from
its broader religious or philosophical connotations, it would cease to
have any power at all. Some groups have of course learned this the
hard way, realizing that the force of their arguments depended on a
rich language not shared in the wider society. The more successful
groups have found ways to integrate specific arguments into a wider
framework of moral understanding, often by drawing heavily from
the symbolism and narrative of religious tradition. Special interest
groups are therefore engaged in public discourse about the sacred
itself, not just about mundane programs concerned with making life
more livable or in some way better.

Special interest groups also color the public perception of the
sacred through the very language they use to impart urgency to
their appeals. Examples of special interest leaders' claiming to have
had divine revelations are not infrequent. Less dramatic appeals also
conjure up images of the sacred. For example, the language of crisis,
sacrifice, moral urgency, and extremes of good and evil often resonate deeply with religious traditions, even if these traditions are not
referenced explicitly. In a society where business is normally conducted in terms of rationality, expedience, and self-interest, these
appeals can stand out as being more closely linked with deep personal convictions and values. It is therefore important to ask about
the contributions special interest groups make not only to substantive issues but also to public understandings of the sacred.

One of the clearest connotations they contribute to public understandings is that the sacred is fundamentally associated with conflict rather than with compromise, consensus, or reconciliation. The
gods worshiped by various special interest groups are of course as
diverse as these groups themselves. In some the divine seems to be
little more than an embarrassing convenience to be paid homage to
during an opening prayer and then forgotten while the tough business of the day is being debated. In others a god of tenderness and
mercy is clearly embodied, at least on the front lines where the needy
are being ministered to compassionately. The public image that has
probably been reinforced more than any other by religious special

interests, however, is one of a wrathful God, who is above all concerned with righteousness, justice, fierce combat against the scourge of evil, and the warriors of good in their fight for God's kingdom. The leaders of religious special interest groups often reinforce this image by using the language of vengeance and of righteous anger in their fund-raising solicitations. Leaders who speak candidly about their groups will also acknowledge that their constituents do not want them to compromise. Were that their aim, they might as well fold up. The argument against compromise, then, is pragmatic and pedagogic. The pragmatic reason for boldly championing a cause is that this is their stated mission and that the group has an obligation to its supporters to pursue this mission. The pedagogic argument is that even if compromise is the eventual result, the group has played a positive function in teaching the public about a particular value, principle, or position.

Whatever the reasons, religious special interest groups have contributed to the broader sense of polarization that currently exists in the religious community. The most visible of these groups have become symbols, not only for a particular position on a single issue but also for an ideological orientation toward a whole cluster of issues. Groups on the extreme political, religious, and moral right have been relatively easy to identify. A few groups have been equally visible on the extreme left. The rhetoric at each extreme has helped push the other into an antagonistic relationship. Much harder to identify are groups in the middle that favor compromise or reconciliation or opt for more creative alternatives on complex social policies. This is not to say that many religious special interest groups do not operate in the middle or without polarizing rhetoric. Many of these groups clearly appeal to narrow constituencies, focus entirely on providing services, or function mainly as professional associations. But these groups have contributed less vocally to the formation of public religion than have the strident groups whose leaders have taken extreme stands on controversial issues of their day.

A second connotation special interest groups give to the sacred is that the divine is scarcely any different from the rational, means-ends, purposive logic that governs other realms of modern society. This connotation follows from what we considered earlier about the rationalized institutional environment in which these groups function. An instrumental orientation is built into the charters of many of these groups and is actualized as they struggle to achieve their stated purposes. This orientation is also evident, as we have seen in previous chapters, in congregations and religious hierarchies. It is probably more extreme in special interest groups, however, for two reasons. Many of these groups, despite a few notable exceptions, operate on extremely tight budgets that are generated by special appeals to accomplish specific goals rather than by appeals for general support or staff salaries. If the group does not pursue its goals concertedly and does not try to achieve them in the most efficient way possible, these funds are likely to disappear. Besides this, special interest groups operate in the most competitive sector of the religious marketplace. Denominational loyalties and neighborhood ties still protect congregations from some of this competition, but special interest groups are never any more secure than the results of their last fund-raising drive. They compete against religious and secular causes of all kinds. If they can prove good use of their resources, they may get more. But let one of their leaders be accused of scandal, or let another issue come on the public scene, and their revenues will diminish overnight. Because of this competition, they must again emphasize how instrumental they are and, in so doing, imply that God loves best those who make things happen.

A third connotation, closely associated with the second, is that the sacred is more concerned with great causes than with other aspects of life. Were archaeologists of some future age to unearth records of the late twentieth century, they would conclude that the gods of this period were especially perplexed by abortion, nuclear weapons, homosexuality, the natural environment, and pornography. The most obedient saints and prophets of this period would undoubtedly be described as those individuals who kept these issues in the public mind. These conclusions would derive mainly from the public pronouncements and literature of religious special interest groups.

Associating the sacred with great causes is perhaps the most distinctive contribution that special interest groups make to the contemporary expression of public religion, for this association runs directly counter to the largely privatized definitions of spirituality that otherwise dominate modern culture. What an archaeologist of the future would soon learn from opinion polls and household records is that most people cared little about the great moral crusades of the twentieth century. They were too busy trying to figure out their own lives to be much affected by these public manifestations of the sacred. Were the question one of public religion, then, the leaders of special interest groups would have to be given much credit indeed. Even if the issue included private spirituality, it might well be that special interest groups made more of an impact than many people realized. If the mass public was not mobilized to fight pornography or nuclear weapons, its constituent members might nevertheless have been troubled sufficiently by these issues to think more deeply about their own spirituality, defining themselves as "more tolerant than leader X" or wishing for the "ethical conviction of leader Y."

Special interest groups are at a disadvantage in producing the sacred when they focus so much attention on practical social programs though. In doing so, they necessarily lose control over much of their own discourse. The special advantage of congregations, especially in the high church or liturgical traditions (and at the extreme fundamentalist end of the theological spectrum), is that they can speak largely in the distinctive language of their own subculture and do so with the authority of specialists who know this language well. The leaders of special interest groups, by comparison, must become experts on particular court cases, bills, or policy proposals. They often do this very well and yet may have no special expertise, especially in comparison with the lawyers, engineers, urban planners, and social welfare experts who claim to know more. What religious leaders can sometimes rely on is the general credibility that the clergy still enjoys relative to politicians, labor organizers, and real estate agents. But this credibility may itself be damaged when the public views clergy not as dispassionate leaders of their flocks but as advocates in the public square. The most serious loss of control over their own discourse, however, comes simply from the fact that religious special interest groups have appeared to react to events in the wider society instead of initiating their own issues. This is still a valuable role for these groups to play. But the *appearance* of being reactive is magnified because they are so often concerned with mobilizing constituents at a distance instead of (as in congregations) simply giving expression to the issues that percolate up from the depths of an intimate community itself.

If they find themselves responding to social issues already placed on the public agenda by other groups, religious special interests can, however, play a very strong role in mobilizing action around those issues by virtue of the lingering power of ideology—even of religious ideology—in secular societies. This power is enhanced by the fact that complex, heterogeneous societies are not the most propitious environments in which to launch programs rooted in material, economic, or political interests alone. Particular individuals, families, or communities are likely to be pulled in a variety of directions because of their multiple roles and interests. To forge any sizable alliance across these different groups, strong rhetoric is therefore likely to be needed.

Challenges and Prospects

The great flurry of activity in which religious special interest groups have been engaged in recent decades suggests that their future may be especially bright as producers of the sacred in modern societies. This activity has been much stronger in the United States than in many other advanced industrial societies. Their relative weakness elsewhere suggests some of the conditions that may work against their being able to exercise cultural influence over the long term.

Perhaps the greatest threat to the activities of special interest groups is simply for centralized bureaucratic agencies to do a better job of orchestrating public policies. These groups flourish in an environment of government and other rationalized organizations, yet they do so because these organizations are loosely coupled, existing more as competitors in an open market than as part of a single, streamlined bureaucracy. Special interest groups have a place in democratic societies because the public still makes a difference in these societies. In totalitarian contexts, where everything is decided behind closed doors, there is little need for special interest groups to mobilize sentiment at all. Even in democratic societies, such as Sweden or Japan, where a small cadre of elected officials make decisions to be implemented by government agencies, the role of special interest groups becomes highly restricted. In the United States these groups play a large role precisely because government agencies often do not function well, or because these agencies farm out many of their tasks to the private sector, and because the system is sufficiently ill-defined to create numerous opportunities for special interests to make a difference. Corruption and conflict are the necessary costs associated with the benefit of giving the public greater access to the reins of power. Were such access denied, religious special interest groups would certainly be among the losers.

Paradoxically, this eventuality is one to which religious groups themselves may inadvertently contribute. As suggested previously, these groups reinforce the idea that formal organization, rational pursuit of limited objectives, and legal rules are the best way to participate in the public arena. They have also been known to champion greater government intrusion in the society in the past, such as providing social security benefits or preventing discrimination against minority groups. Religious groups especially need to be mindful that government control is not always the best solution to social problems. It may be necessary where large public expenditures must be mandated or where equal treatment for all citizens is required, but religious groups that talk as if legislation or considerations of rights and justice were the only thing that matters are giving up much of the richness of their own traditions. Forgiveness, mercy, and compassion may not be concepts highly valued on Capitol Hill, but they may be among the most powerful tools available to religious communities.

The relative success of special interest groups may also be their worst enemy in another way. Commitment to these groups, it appears, generally is quite high among a relatively small cadre of leaders and activists, evokes periodic attention from a larger clientele, and fails to generate anything but apathy from the wider public. Yet the wider public continues to register interest in spirituality in much more personalized ways. Should churches and religious leaders become too obsessed with great social causes, they are likely to cut themselves off from the very basis of their grass-roots support. The danger is always that too much emphasis on public religion can rob it of its vital connection with private spirituality. When that happens, erosion of public religion itself is likely to follow.

What augurs best for the continued vitality of religious special interest groups is that they, perhaps more than any of the other organizational forms we have considered, function in a dynamic competitive market. The fortunes of any particular group may wax and wane, but in the larger scheme of things there is always room for new groups to emerge. When established groups cease making a notable impact on the public sphere, they may not actually die, but their continued existence may be bought at relatively low cost because their resources are so closely related to the scope of their activities. Meanwhile, potential constituents can turn their attention to new causes. Special interest groups are, in this sense, especially well suited to a diverse and changing social environment. This is the kind of environment they are most likely to experience in the years ahead.

5

Academies

Academies have always been among the most significant means by which religious institutions sought to influence the beliefs and values of their host societies. At one time virtually all formal education was carried out by organizations under religious sponsorship. Schools, colleges, and seminaries supplemented the religious instruction provided by families and local churches. Today these organizations' social role has been greatly attenuated by the growth of public education and the rise of secular colleges and universities. Religiously sponsored academies nevertheless remain an important vehicle for shaping and transmitting fundamental human values.

As contributors to the production of public discourse about the sacred, church-related institutions of higher education are by far the most influential type of religiously sponsored academies. Church-related colleges provide the crucibles in which new ideas can be articulated and debated, connecting confessional traditions with topics of contemporary relevance and exposing young adults to these ideas during a critical phase of their intellectual development. Church-related colleges also play an important public role in supporting scholars, who in turn contribute to wider intellectual discussions through their publications, participation in conferences, lay leadership positions in churches and community organizations, and commentary on public events in the mass media. Church-sponsored elementary and secondary schools, by comparison, generally play a less direct role in the shaping of public discourse, influencing the beliefs and values of children who only later become active participants in the public arena.

Because the role of church-related academies has been diminished by the growth of secular alternatives, it is also important for us to consider colleges and universities of this wider variety. At secular institutions of higher learning understandings of the sacred may be infused into the public arena through the specialized work of faculty in religious studies departments, through the teaching and research of individual faculty in other disciplines who happen to be interested in religion, and through the numerous chaplaincies, campus ministries, and parachurch organizations that work directly with students.

The Resources of Academies

The resources that give academies the opportunity to produce public discourse about the sacred fall into two categories: those that contribute to the general goals of colleges and universities and those that affect the specific place of religion within these organizations. The former have for the most part been on the increase over the past century or more, while the latter have shown a mixed pattern.

The overall work of colleges and universities depends greatly on the presence in virtually all modernized societies—and in most developing societies as well—of a value structure that legitimates higher education. So pervasive is this legitimacy that its significance can easily be overlooked. Middle-class parents save more seriously for their children's college education than for anything else, with the exception of their homes. Moreover, it is inconceivable to imagine that the taxpayers in places like California or New York would fund anything else on the same scale that they do the public university systems established in those states. To say that colleges and universities depend on a favorable value structure is thus to suggest something more than a subjective predisposition to recognize the importance of higher education. These values take on objective stature in the budgets of families and state administrators. They are also a pervasive aspect of the public culture, manifested in the mass media and in history books as well. Children grow up knowing that higher education is an integral feature of the adult world, much in the same way they probably knew that about the church in medieval societies.

Values are nevertheless of little significance in the case of higher education except for the fact that in such modern societies as the

United States there is also the economic wherewithal to make good on these values. The fact that middle-class parents can afford to pay amounts equivalent to a quarter or more of their family incomes for annual college tuition payments is evidence of the margin for discretionary expenditures that exists in these societies. Affluence is one of the environmental conditions on which the current system of colleges and universities greatly depends.

The economy is, however, more integrally related to higher education than being simply a source of external support. Higher education is generally thought to feed resources back into the economy, and this relation is so complex that secondary systems of reward and social status have also become closely linked with the attainment of advanced education. Part of what legitimates vast social expenditures on higher education is the assumption that these funds actually constitute an investment in the future, an expense that will reap high dividends, both for the society at large and for the individuals directly involved. Higher education is justified in utilitarian cost-benefit analyses in ways that expenses on, say, religious institutions seldom can be. In addition, higher education has become a major determinant of social status and the numerous life-style differences associated with the stratification system. Entry into various occupations is heavily contingent on having attained the appropriate educational credentials, a fact that becomes all the more significant when other criteria, including ethnic origins and "creeds," have been made illegitimate in most societies. Even on such private matters as choice of marital partners, similar educational levels have risen in importance relative to such traditional criteria as national, regional, and religious homophyly.

All these broader conditions would still be of little importance were it not for the organizational resources that have been amassed over the decades by colleges and universities themselves. These include the evolution of the professorate as a legitimate occupational choice; the gradual development of a significant segment of the labor force trained to occupy positions within the professoriat; methods of certifying the professional status of—and restricting entry into—these positions; and a relatively stable system of rankings, divisions of knowledge into academic disciplines, and the organization of colleges and universities into schools and departments. These organizational resources are largely taken for granted on a day-to-day basis, yet many of them scarcely existed a century ago, and many are still subject to ongoing discussion and modification at colleges and universities around the country.

Any review of the resources on which colleges and universities depend would also be incomplete if it failed to mention the role of the state. On the surface it is obvious that a large share of the funding for higher education now comes from public sources. The state is, however, a critical factor in orchestrating a favorable climate for higher education more generally. Just as Max Weber pointed out in tracing the conditions favorable to the rise of capitalism in the West, so we might emphasize that long-term political stability has been a significant element in the development of higher education. Regimes that have tried to control higher education too closely or have intimidated scholars to the point of causing them to emigrate, or even regimes that led their populations into costly and destructive wars, have contributed negatively to the evolution of colleges and universities. These examples also attest to the importance of political and legal respect for traditions of academic freedom, not to mention the positive encouragement given to higher education by politically motivated competition between states and foreign powers or between political units within the same national arena. The current competition between the United States and Japan to support effective systems of higher education has a long precedent in similar competitions between France and Germany in the nineteenth century or between Scottish and Dutch universities at an earlier date. Even the competition between such universities as Ohio State and Indiana University is rooted in political divisions and has consequences quite similar to those that resulted in the growth of a national system of universities in the German territories during the last century.

Finally, it is worth mentioning the broader system of supportive organizations on which colleges and universities depend. Like any business firm, a college or university does not exist in a vacuum but carries out its activities in connection with numerous subcontractors and supplemental organizations. These include national testing organizations, without which the complex decisions surrounding recruitment and selection of students would be impossible; the professional associations to which faculty members belong; publishing companies that produce textbooks; insurance companies; alumni groups; the military; and hosts of other academic suppliers.

All these resources contribute to the overall prominence of higher education in modern societies. Without these resources colleges and universities would be unable to carry out their stated educational aims and would have a smaller impact on the public sphere more generally. A reduction in any of these resources might also affect the likelihood that colleges and universities would be able to infuse ideas about religion into the public arena. That likelihood, however, also depends on some resources concerned more specifically with the role of religion in higher education. Some of these resources—for example, the overall strength of denominational hierarchies capable of supplying financial support to church-related colleges, or a political system that respects the right of religious organizations to operate in the educational sphere—are relatively straightforward, but the role of others is sometimes counterintuitive.

One example of this kind of resource is the role played by the First Amendment to the U.S. Constitution in encouraging or discouraging religion within American higher education. It has been argued that separation of church and state has worked to the disadvantage of religion in higher education because public monies were thereby denied to organizations advancing the cause of religion. It has also been argued, however, that such separation played a positive role in that it prevented government from restricting religious activities and encouraged voluntary contributions to religion in higher education, just as it did to the churches more generally. Contradictory as these two arguments may seem, the truth is that both are probably correct. The combination of circumstances suggested by both arguments probably contributed most to the present state of religion in American higher education. Separation of church and state has often posed a challenge for church-related colleges or for those wishing to include religious offerings on secular campuses. It presented enough of a challenge to encourage voluntary support for private church-related colleges and campus ministries adjacent to secular campuses. It was by no means draconian in its execution, however. Government officials have for the most part loosely interpreted the First Amendment, permitting public monies to be granted to church-related colleges for, say, building dormitories, supporting individual students under the National Defense Education Act, or sponsoring scientific research. What is probably of greatest significance is the fact that the relation between church and state was thus fraught with uncertainty. Religious activities could benefit at times from government sponsorship, yet this support was always sufficiently unpredictable that those most interested in religion were unwilling to let their activities become entirely dependent on such funding.

A similar argument can probably be made concerning the much-noted ambivalence of religious organizations themselves toward higher education. On the one hand, most of the old-line Protestant denominations and the Catholic church have been responsible for the founding of numerous private colleges and universities. On the other hand, the administrators and faculties of these institutions of higher learning often found themselves in tension with their supporting ecclesiastical entities, feeling themselves pressured to take stands on issues that defied reason or compromised their intellectual integrity, and these misgivings were often justified by the presence of trustees or denominational administrators who wanted to channel higher education toward their own purposes or who were fundamentally suspicious of the academic life in the first place. The result was a kind of uncertainty, much like that inspired by the varying interpretations of the First Amendment, and this uncertainty encouraged the various actors to seek mutually beneficial relations wherever possible and yet to maintain the relative autonomy of their respective institutions. In the larger scheme of things, religious ideas at many church-related colleges and universities may have been better facilitated through this arrangement than if denominational leaders had had complete control or no control at all.

The other resource that has perhaps had similar consequences for the role of religion in higher education is the cultural division of knowledge into disciplinary categories. This division has, on the one hand, resulted in a kind of intellectual fragmentation and even warfare that has often been decried by religionists who favor closer integration between, say, theology and science or religion and the arts. The same division, on the other hand, has made it possible for ideas in these various realms to be pursued intensively in a way that would likely have been compromised had cross-disciplinary connections always been necessary. The clearest example of this positive benefit of disciplinary specialization is the fact that practitioners of the natural sciences, in which the scientific paradigm is most clearly articulated, are much more likely to retain deep personal religious convictions than are practitioners of the social sciences and the humanities, in which both the internal paradigm and external boundaries defining each discipline are less clearly articulated.

The upshot of these counterintuitive considerations is that gloomy assertions about the long-term decline of religion within higher education are probably overstated. Certainly, compared with the cultural climate of five hundred years ago, the overall cultural climate in contemporary societies may be more heavily influenced by secular higher education than by the church. But the rising influence of higher education, even in its most secular forms, has also opened new opportunities for religion to influence the public sphere as part of the legitimate activities associated with colleges and universities. In addition, cultural boundaries restricting the role of religion and demarcating the sacred from the secular have not always had purely negative implications for the public expression of the sacred. It is for this reason that religious activities within the academic realm have developed, not in any uniform pattern but according to a variety of organizational forms.

Variations in Organizational Patterns

Were we to engage in some massive utopian experiment in biological engineering, we would find that developing an animal species to inhabit a complex, heterogeneous, and uncertain social environment of the kind we have just described would probably require creating not just one species but a whole variety of species that could seek out different niches in that environment and adapt more readily to changing circumstances. That is in fact what has happened in higher education. As this arena has expanded, becoming an increasingly significant part of the complex environment of modern societies, its own organizational forms and the role of religion within these organizations have become increasingly varied. The development of junior colleges, vocational-technical schools, advanced degrees, interdisciplinary programs, and research centers illustrates this variation in the wider context of American higher education. The complex menu of church-related colleges, campus ministries, religious studies departments, and parachurch organizations to which I alluded earlier suggests some of the variation pertaining specifically to religious activities.

The dimensions along which the variation in colleges and universities is generally classified include auspices (public or private), function (ranging from multipurpose research and teaching institutions to more specialized organizations), level of prestige, and size. In combination these dimensions describe the complex patterns into which American institutions of higher education are generally divided (for example, a public, multipurpose research university with high prestige and many students, such as UCLA, at one extreme, and a private, specialized college with relatively low prestige and few students, such as Philadelphia Bible College, at the other extreme). How particular organizations are located along these various dimensions has important implications for the ways in which they may contribute to the public expression of religion. Before considering those implications, however, three observations about the dimensions themselves are worthy of attention.

First, colleges and universities are subject to tendencies that cause them to differentiate along these dimensions, yet there are also countervailing tendencies generating organizational uniformity along other dimensions. The differentiating tendencies are driven primarily by competition that leads particular institutions to occupy specialized roles in the larger social environment. For example, a single metropolitan area of a hundred thousand people may be able to sustain a large public university, a community college, and a private church-related college, but the same area probably would not be able to sustain three large public universities. The countertendencies, though, are equally important. In a complex environment they help identify organizations of varying sizes or functions as nevertheless being part of the same academic domain. All three of the organizations just mentioned, for example, would probably have in common a president, a board of trustees, a curriculum, a published catalog, a library, a student association, a health service, not to mention a host of other similarities. Some of these common features may be required by law (a board of trustees), others are part of the culturally accepted definition of an educational institution (a curriculum), and still others may be matters of sheer imitation (a student association). These commonalities will be important to consider when we turn specifically to religious activities.

Second, the dimensions along which colleges and universities vary represent real distinctions (say, in numbers of students) but are themselves culturally defined systems of classification. This is most evident in the case of prestige rankings—which are often quite subjective or at least based on highly arbitrary criteria—but it is true even of functional and sponsorship distinctions. What distinguishes a research university from a college is often quite arbitrary. The resulting arbitrariness of classifications is important in its own right (as we shall see momentarily), but it is also worth noting that different subcultures can define these classifications differently. While there may be a standard prestige rating published by accrediting associations, a very different ranking may exist among the members of a particular religious denomination or among people living in a local community. What constitutes "private" or "research" or "small" may also vary according to the audience.

The third point follows from the second: none of these distinctions is clean. Public and private is perhaps the least arbitrary distinction, yet a public university like UCLA may have such a large private endowment that it functions at times more like the latter, or a university like Cornell may actually be divided into a public part and a private part. Similar complexities may exist in formally designated private colleges concerning whether they are church-related or nonsectarian. Such complexities greatly add to the diversity of arrangements by which religious values are expressed through institutions of higher learning.

Moving to a consideration of the implications of these variations for religious expression, it is generally argued that the growth of public higher education at the expense of private colleges and universities has been the most consequential development for the academic representation of religious values. Over roughly the past half-century the balance of enrollments and economic resources has certainly shifted in that direction. Public higher education has enjoyed an enormous advantage by virtue of its access to tax monies for support, while private organizations, especially church-related colleges, have suffered severely as a result of constitutional provisions against the public support of religious causes. The result has been an overall decline in the proportion of higher educational institutions offering courses from a particular confessional perspective or claiming to uphold particular religious traditions. Yet the more significant result has probably been a net increase in the ways in which religious beliefs and values are made public.

This increase stems partly from the stimulating effect that the growth of public higher education has had on private colleges and universities. As the one grew, so did the other, at least in absolute terms. Even church-related colleges increased in size and number because public institutions were not always conveniently located and because religiously minded parents still preferred to send their off-spring to these colleges. This growth was often facilitated not only by generous private giving, stimulated by the rising cultural legiti-macy of higher education in general, but also by grants-in-aid from the federal government itself.

In addition, diversity increased in both the public and private sec-tors because each type of institution found multiple ways to accom-modate the growth facing it. Private colleges became infinitely more diverse in size, prestige, and functions (compare the present diversity with that in colonial America). Those that sought to become presti-gious research and teaching institutions often shed their denomina-tional affiliations but retained chaplaincies and informal ties between academic and church boards, while other colleges defined themselves ever more ardently in religious terms against these secularizing ten-dencies. At public institutions, faculty and student interest in reli-gion also remained sufficient to find ways around formal rules ex-cluding the teaching of religion. Rather than teach religion, courses were designed to teach "about" religion, churches or campus minis-tries were founded on property adjacent to colleges and universities under private auspices, and student religious organizations were ini-tiated on the model of fraternities and sororities or athletic clubs.

The increasing *functional* differentiation of colleges and universi-ties also went hand in hand with the growth of public higher educa-tion; large multipurpose research universities and technical colleges alike proliferated primarily under public auspices. As research and technical competence became more important, the teaching of reli-gious values again suffered a relative decline. Knowledge, critics ar-gued, became more compartmentalized, and standards of empiricism and efficiency began to edge out consideration of more fundamen-tal human values. This was only part of the picture, though. Again, increasing organizational variety also contributed to the diversity of means by which religious values could be expressed. Although the multipurpose research university has risen dramatically in im-portance since World War II, it has seldom replaced the idea of an integrated liberal arts education at the undergraduate level. Relatively few genuinely graduate, research-oriented universities have been founded; the majority have instead attempted to combine the traditional college education with advanced training and research.

For religion the result has been twofold: the retention of some kind of course offering in religion at the undergraduate level and more specialized graduate-level research and training in religion or related subjects. In theory at least, the holistic vision embodied in the classic liberal arts ideal, in which religious and human values were an integral part of the educational experience, has been retained at the undergraduate level, while opportunities for more specialized work have also been made available. More broadly, the same diversity is often evident in private secular colleges, in church-related colleges with graduate components, and in more specialized Bible colleges.

The stratification of American colleges and universities into a prestige hierarchy has also had mixed consequences for the public expression of religion through these organizations. Few of the highly prestigious institutions of higher learning have retained close affiliations with sponsoring religious bodies (although there are some notable exceptions). The criteria on which prestige is based are themselves increasingly composed of standards that may run counter to such confessional affiliations—the availability of research monies from public sources, large private endowments from a religiously pluralistic constituency, recruitment of the most academically qualified students without respect to creed, and so on. As a result, church-related colleges have come to suffer a certain (perhaps self-perpetuating) stigma in wider academic circles, and this stigma has sometimes encouraged faculty and students at these institutions to adopt an antimodern, antiliberal, or antimainstream orientation toward public affairs. At the same time, the few church-related colleges and universities that have competed successfully for national prestige—for example, the University of Notre Dame or Brigham Young University—have contributed positively to the public image of their respective faith traditions and have probably assisted these traditions in their efforts to shape public values. At secular colleges and universities, high academic prestige has sometimes performed a similar image-enhancing role for the student religious organizations that function on these campuses. Holding a large Campus Crusade for Christ rally at the University of California, Berkeley, for example, is fundamentally different from holding the same rally at the overpass campus of Eastern California State Technical College.

The differentiation of colleges and universities by size has perhaps been one of the most consequential developments for the public expression of religion through institutions of higher learning. Prior to the 1960s few campuses touted sizable enrollments, and the vast majority continued to recruit students from their immediate regions. The infusion of vast sums of federal, state, and local funds into higher education in the 1960s and 1970s, together with more college-age young people because of the so-called baby boom, resulted in the relatively rapid growth of megauniversities, with student enrollments in the tens of thousands, and the rise of many new campuses. The same growth allowed many struggling church-related colleges to reach a level of operation that ensured their survival for the foreseeable future. The single issue appearing in all these contexts was a concern for community—or, as it was often described, cultivating a form of "student life" that overcame the anonymity of the mega-campus and provided genuinely nurturing social relationships for the typical student.

Religious leaders responded aggressively to this challenge. Among its other functions the church had always sought to provide community, and growing numbers of Sunday school and youth programs in the 1950s had given it some confidence in its ability to do so for college students as well. Even confessions that were uncertain of their theological emphases in the 1960s found that community was an issue they could champion, especially when it could be linked with other agendas, such as civil rights, urban ministries, and social activism. Because the organizational contexts were so varied, however, religious bodies attempted to provide community on campuses in widely differing ways. At the larger colleges and universities vast numbers of students made it possible for more specialized ministries to be initiated. A Danforth Chapel or a chapter of Inter-Varsity Christian Fellowship, for example, could be founded more easily on a campus of ten thousand than on a campus of a thousand. At small colleges, in contrast, smallness itself suddenly became a virtue; what these colleges lacked in diversity of course offerings was said to be outweighed by the more intimate, personalized campus atmosphere. Church-related colleges often seized on this argument, sometimes claiming to provide a wholesome, congenial environment in which like-minded students could interact and sometimes promising parents that their offspring could be more closely supervised.

Currently, then, colleges and universities provide a highly varied set of organizational means by which to infuse religious values into the public sphere. This variation is to a considerable degree a function of the rapid growth that higher education has undergone during the past quarter-century and of the programs that developed during these decades to adapt religious life to the campus environment. That many different programs were initiated was on balance a positive development, because the fortunes of some could wane and yet religious values could still be fostered by others. By the end of the 1970s many of the denominationally sponsored campus ministries that had been started in the 1960s had fallen on hard times, yet parachurch organizations and religious studies programs had grown in prominence. Despite their overall diversity, religious programs in American higher education have been constrained in their capacity to manifest the sacred; at the same time they have enjoyed certain advantages, simply by virtue of their association with the campus environment.

How the Sacred Is Produced

It is easy enough to enumerate the various programs, ministries, courses, publishing activities, and the like by which religious values are made public through institutions of higher learning, yet to understand the nature of this process we must ask other questions. How are these values shaped by their being produced in the context of higher learning? What gives them an appearance of being sacred? How do they interact with other values that may also embody a sense of the sacred? We can seek answers to these questions by considering how the academic context constrains the public expression of the sacred and how this context also facilitates these expressions.

One of the most serious constraints on expressions of the sacred within academic contexts is the separation of reason from emotion and from action that generally characterizes institutions of higher learning. This separation reflects the lingering dualistic epistemology of the Enlightenment that presumes knowledge to be gained best by objectifying the world, viewing it as an externality, instead of attempting to appropriate it subjectively (or internally) through the counsels of feeling or through wisdom gained from direct action. While there have been significant philosophical challenges in the twentieth century to this perspective, it certainly prevails in secular and church-related colleges and universities alike. Understanding may be enriched by subjective identification with the object or by the intuitive insight gained through direct participation, but the goal is still to gain knowledge that can be understood cognitively and communicated rationally.

Knowledge gained this way presents a special limitation for public expressions of the sacred, for such knowledge comes across as having too little to do with the full life of the individual. Passion, trust, conviction, faith, and devotion are all subordinated to dispassionate statements about the facts or truths of a world viewed as it were from outside. It is little wonder, then, that church bureaucrats concerned with running institutions on the basis of rationally devised technical considerations have more frequently turned to the studies and methods of academicians (especially in the social sciences) than have people in the pew who are trying to integrate faith into the full measure of their lives. For these people, the words of a priest who has struggled with the same issues are likely to be meaningful in a way that an objective study of religious institutions can never be.

This observation lends some credence to the view that scholarly approaches to religion are inevitably corrosive, contributing in subtle ways to the larger processes of secularization. For the believer, depersonalized knowledge presented in scholarly texts is likely to seem alien, setting up a boundary between such knowledge (viewed as public information) and the more private insights that govern his or her spiritual life. The spiritual realm is thus increasingly segmented from public discourse, leaving it to hold mastery over only the private or subjective realm. For the nonbeliever who already approaches spirituality as a stranger looking in from the outside, depersonalized knowledge (such as a study of religious belief reported in the newspapers) can further enhance this estrangement by objectifying the religious realm and associating it with the other primarily through intellect.

A second but related limitation of higher education in producing the sacred derives from the tension between what might be called creation, on the one hand, and discovery, on the other hand. Creation implies invention, novelty, the development of something new that in a deep sense reflects the talents and insights of the creator. Discovery, in contrast, implies paying close attention to the external world, grasping it as a given reality, so that what is new is only a description of what has always been there. Western religion has always distinguished the two by attributing creation to a divine being who is the author or originator of all reality, whereas discovery is more likely to be described as a human activity, such as learning to understand better the nature of created reality or gaining insight into the darker recesses of one's own nature.

At the dawn of the scientific revolution the work of scientists was well described as an act of discovery. Natural laws inscribed in the world by its creator were there for the finding, just as new continents had been there a century earlier for the explorers. Academic work was in fact likened to reading a text—in one case the text might still be the written Bible; in other cases it was the word of God written in nature. Reportage of academic discoveries was thus largely a matter of communicating knowledge of a sacred realm that was already in place. This congruity between academic work and the sacred served well to legitimate the religious sponsorship of higher learning in church-related academies and the close connections that were drawn between moral philosophy and natural philosophy in secular institutions.

The present understanding of academic work, however, has shifted decidedly away from discovery toward creation itself. Artistic expression, in which a product is created that reflects the moods and interests of the artist, is perhaps the clearest model of this understanding. Increasingly, science imitates art in this respect, as measuring devices are known to alter the very realities they seek to measure, and as theoretical inventions are understood to alter the very possibilities of perceiving reality. The most highly valued academic work, therefore, is the creative process by which new ideas, new theories, or even new ways of expressing ideas are invented; by comparison, discovery is increasingly relegated to the realm of empiricism, factmongering, and technical specialization.

The limitation that this conception of academic work presents for the discussion of religion is that God remains fundamentally an entity to be discovered rather than one to be invented. Scriptural exegesis becomes a process of discovering insights within a closely circumscribed field of textual meanings and applying these insights to changing circumstances. Going beyond discovery to create an entirely new conception of God is, however, to move beyond the pale of most confessional traditions. The resultant strain between these two modes of understanding reveals itself, therefore, either as heterodoxy confronting orthodoxy or as more highly valued creative expressions confronting the less highly valued processes of textual interpretation.

The main consequence of these two limitations — depersonalized reason and the devaluation of discovery — for the public expression of religion through academic organizations is that academicians tend to talk about religion in ways that are seldom valued highly within their institutions themselves, while the most creative contributions to spirituality come largely from outside these institutions. What a typical layperson might read in the newspapers would thus be a report of an academic study of the religious beliefs of the American population, but this reader would not expect to learn that a fundamental new theory of God had been produced or that the authors of such a report had won a Nobel Prize for their efforts. Nor would this reader be likely to rely on such a report for guidance in his or her own attempts to seek God. Higher credence would be given to a playwright who wrote from the deep anguish of having been imprisoned by a totalitarian government, a recovering alcoholic who had struggled with the depths of personal pain, or in the rare instance an academic marginal to any specific department or discipline who wrote from personal reflection more than from systematic empirical inquiry.

Part of the reason why public discourse about the sacred would be shaped more deeply by nonacademics than by academics, if this argument is correct, is that higher learning has erected a boundary not only between reason and emotion but also between knowledge and moral discourse. The public pronouncements of academicians are more likely to take the form of descriptive statements than that of normative prescriptions, in part because of the way in which the role of the academy has come to be understood in modern societies. This role involves a deliberate retreat from active engagement in public life to protect the purity of scholarship itself. It also grants ultimate authority for the manipulation of social structures to government organizations, taking only a detached advisory role in policymaking. The fact that government in democratic societies generally refrains from intruding on the private decisions of individuals, however, leaves a large realm untutored either by government or by the academy. This realm, often described as personal morality, has always been subject to the pronouncements of religious institutions, either at the level of congregations or hierarchies. When these organizations functioned with cultural authority and higher education consisted mainly of church-related organizations, a natural division of labor existed that allowed the academies to focus (in the best circumstances) on moral philosophy rather than on concrete moral prescriptions. With the erosion of the churches' authority over the lives of many people in modern societies, however, a gap has been created in moral discourse that seems to be filled by common sense, ad hoc and situational reasoning, television, and other purveyors of moral fiction more than by institutions of higher learning.

Instead of simply attributing this failure on the part of academicians to address moral issues to a lack of nerve or shortsightedness of vision, however, we must try to understand it in terms of the kind of authority modern culture confers on academicians. Their authority as culture producers inheres mainly in the special advantages assumed to derive from specialized, critical reflection. The point of academic institutions is, after all, to provide opportunities for such reflection, and the fact that resources flow to these institutions both reinforces and attests to the legitimacy such reflection has acquired. Scholars interested in religious and moral questions are thus most likely to be given credence for analytic and critical studies. Taking their cue from the natural sciences, they may try to understand how the sacred functions—why it works or does not work—but in analyzing the divine in this way, they are more likely to recognize that they are examining human assumptions about God instead of observing God directly. Their authority as dispassionate scholars is also likely to encourage critical orientations rather than the sort of celebrations of the divine one might expect from a liturgist or a poet.

Scholars' views of nature also suggest another limitation on the kind of authoritative knowledge they may be able to produce about the sacred. These views are heavily oriented toward technical mastery and manipulation. The rationale for much of the funding that goes toward applied research, and even for basic science, is that the knowledge gained will help us better control the physical environment. The prospect of government's being able to engage in social engineering has encouraged a similar technical orientation in the social sciences, and even in the humanities much of what passes for historical studies and literary criticism has a manipulative orientation either in the sense of better mastering the future by knowing the past or in discovering the techniques by which meaning can be created and deciphered in literature. At one time, of course, the shamans who preceded modern academicians concerned themselves largely with the technical manipulation of the gods, but in modern societies this technical orientation is largely in disrepute. Scholars may legitimately concern themselves with manipulating nature but not God. That function has thus been given over to the various television preachers, prayer warriors, and mediums who claim specialized talents in influencing the divine. Academicians, as we have observed, are more likely to contribute to public discourse about the manipulation of religious institutions than of the sacred itself.

One other limitation of the academy deserving mention is that the secular knowledge it produces is often shrouded in such sacred conceptions that this knowledge—as well as its pursuit—takes the place of religious conviction. Anyone familiar with the capital fund-raising drives and alumni relations of colleges and universities will immediately grasp this point. Institutions of higher learning symbolize a sacred space—the navel of the world—where truth is closer, where the mundane concerns of business and family can be bracketed from view, where athletic prowess and physical beauty are at their peak, and where the youthfulness even of aging professors and alumni can safely be preserved. If the pursuit of knowledge is in some way a sacred quest, it is all the more so because of the special places (we call them "hallowed halls") in which learning takes place. Religious congregations have an advantage over these institutions insofar as they are able to lay down the foundational values learned in early childhood, but higher education enjoys an enormous competitive advantage over congregations in being able to capture the full attention of young people just when they are questioning their childhood values and adopting the ideas they will carry into adulthood. When religious ideas are fully integrated into the formal and hidden curricula of the campus, this advantage can work to the benefit of public religion. Studies documenting negative relations between the attainment of higher education and the retention of religious convictions suggest a different pattern, however. Campuses may de-legitimate religion by subjecting it to critical reason and sanctifying alternative values, such as relativism, the pursuit of secular knowledge for its own sake, or even raw careerism, narrow professionalism, and crass materialism.

These limitations notwithstanding, the campus environment also enjoys certain features that contribute positively to the public expression of the sacred. One of the most important of these is the atmosphere of open, unrestrained intellectual inquiry that is often associated with higher education. Just how open this atmosphere actually is has been questioned repeatedly in recent years, especially by critics who argue that higher education is dominated by a subtle, but powerful, liberal ideology that prevents genuine consideration of politically or religiously conservative perspectives. Compared with many other institutional settings, the academic environment has a relatively strong norm against imposing explicit ideological tests on the activities of those engaged in serious intellectual pursuits. The upshot is that students and faculty often find the academy a more conducive setting in which to engage in frank explorations of religious values than virtually anyplace else. In contrast the same person may feel uncomfortable in a congregational setting because certain answers are assumed to be precluded from the outset or because clergy function not only as spiritual guides but as commandeers of volunteer labor and charitable donations. Secular campuses probably convey the image of being most open to exploring issues, including religious ones, from all angles with nothing other than genuine intellectual integrity at stake, although this image often does fall short of reality because of ingrained prejudices against the value of faith or the wisdom of religious traditions themselves. Church-related campuses may preclude some of the freedom to explore from all possible angles because of their loyalty to particular traditions, yet this limitation may be more than compensated for by the seriousness with which the religious life itself is taken.

In attempting to communicate the results of these explorations to the wider public, scholars in these various settings are also likely to experience similar advantages and disadvantages. The main advantage accruing to the scholar in a secular academic setting is that whatever conclusions the scholar chooses to publicize may be accorded the respect that comes with a presumably objective approach. The disadvantage is that a deeply impassioned plea framed in confessional language by such a scholar is likely to earn trouble for that person within the academy itself. For scholars at church-related colleges, the obverse is likely to pertain: trust may be granted only by an audience sharing the same confessional tradition, but speaking passionately from this tradition is less likely to be regarded as a breech of academic norms.

The technical or applied knowledge mentioned earlier also gives institutions of higher learning some clear advantages in influencing the shape of religious institutions. Scholars may find it beyond their legitimate roles to invent new gods or manipulate existing gods, but they can produce knowledge that the leaders of religious hierarchies take seriously enough to influence the direction of these hierarchies. Studies of how the churches promoted anti-Semitism were at one point influential in encouraging church leaders to adopt different official policies toward Jews. Studies in more recent years documenting that congregations were able to accept women in clergy roles have been instrumental in encouraging denominational leaders to champion gender equality in the churches.

Challenges and Prospects

If we ask what kind of contribution colleges and universities can make to the public expression of religion, one obvious answer is that academic knowledge can play a valuable technical role. Such knowledge will probably not capture the imaginations and hearts of pious individuals, but it will be of interest to the leaders of institutions who shape the goals of churches or public policy toward the churches. Knowledge of this kind is unlikely to earn the high respect that more creative contributions in the natural sciences and the arts are likely to receive, but its social and cultural impact may be considerable. The reason for this is that, as we have seen in previous chapters, conceptions of the sacred are very much a function of the institutions that produce them. These conceptions, in short, are cultural products and, unlike the weather or some feature of physical geography, are therefore subject to the shaping power of cultural institutions. Academic knowledge helps, in turn, to guide these institutions. It plays an archival role, if nothing else, preserving the past so that religious institutions can know more easily if they have strayed from or remained true to this past. Academic knowledge also functions as a mirror in which religious leaders can view themselves and their activities. It may not tell them what to do, but it can help them correct their course should they so desire.

The greatest challenge in public religion to which academic knowledge can respond positively is the growing level of religious and cultural pluralism in modern societies. Although pluralism has sometimes been thought to lead inevitably to greater secularity, the future of religion in pluralistic societies is probably more indeterminate than that view would suggest. Pluralism can stimulate competition among religious traditions, and it can be layered into deeper personal religious convictions as well. Academic knowledge has for several centuries advanced the cause of cultural pluralism, claiming to present a more enlightened vantage point than that available in any particular tradition and championing egalitarianism, mutual respect, and the search for shared values among pluralistic subcultures. Academic knowledge has continuously been put forth in universalistic terms said to be relevant and applicable in a wide variety of settings.

Arguments couched in universalistic language serve a vital function in public discourse about collective values. Indeed, it might be argued that the chief role academies can play in expressing public religion is that of arbiter or translator, framing arguments in detached, externalist terms so they can be understood and debated across a wide spectrum of confessional traditions. Congregations, denominational hierarchies, and religious special interest groups may also do this in their efforts to reach pluralistic audiences, but academies are in a better position to do so because they do not have to speak from the perspective of any particular religious tradition. Church-related colleges are of course somewhat more constrained in this than are secular institutions of higher learning, but many church-related colleges have been able to devise charters giving themselves sufficient autonomy from host denominations that faculty and students still have relatively wide latitude in exploring intellectual questions. Academicians in both types of settings have the cultural authority to raise critical questions and to pose religious issues in broader—historical, cross-cultural, and cross-confessional —terms so that these issues can genuinely become part of the wider public culture. Being able to speak *about* religious language, instead of having to speak in religious language itself, is of special value when competing religious arguments are at issue.

On balance, then, the view that colleges and universities necessarily are subject to, and contributors to, a secularized public culture seems mistaken, as does the view that colleges and universities must tighten their ties to sponsoring religious bodies if they are going to resist these secularizing pressures. Secularization misconstrues the question because it suggests a linear trend away from something definably religious toward something patently nonreligious. A more compelling view of the changes taking place in modern societies is one that recognizes the simultaneous interplay of the sacred and the secular. Colleges and universities have contributed significantly — and will continue to contribute — to this interplay. They are among the chief producers of secular knowledge, but they also provide valuable enclaves in which special types of religious knowledge can be produced and preserved.

6

Public Ritual

Writing a half-century ago in his celebrated study of Yankee City, the sociologist W. Lloyd Warner concluded that public ritual was one of the primary ways in which the sacred is produced and commemorated in American communities. In our holidays and festivities the name of God is exalted and brought into a close relation with our collective purposes. The community is drawn together, each segment brings its distinctive past into the public arena, common heroes and shared values are remembered, citizens are connected in sacred bonds with their families and neighbors, and the ordinary rhythms of community life are put in tune with the sacred harmonies of the universe. Public ritual is a way of producing talk about the sacred that connects it with our collective history and our identity as a people.

Of all the public rituals he studied, Warner was most interested in those associated with Memorial Day, for in these services the living and the dead joined together in the most fundamental sacred rites of all. Weeks of preparation were involved. Memorial Day services were clearly an example of cultural production. The American Legion, Veterans of Foreign Wars, descendants of the Grand Old Army of the Republic, and all the churches in the small New England town of Yankee City planned a full day of ceremonies that included the selling and wearing of poppies, the placing of flags in cemeteries, sermons, public gatherings at local cemeteries, and a parade in which all the voluntary organizations in the town were represented. All these events were deeply infused with the language of God. Each group worshiped in its own way but found unity because all were remembering their dead and the values for which they died.

The Memorial Day rituals that Warner described still exist today in small towns across the country. Attending these rituals, one gains a subjective understanding of why they work. Here, riding in a vintage 1949 Packard, come two wizened veterans of World War II. We know one because he attends our church; the other ran the hardware store before he retired. As they pass we can see the pride in their eyes and feel indebted to them for the bravery they once displayed. We remember our uncle who gave his life on Iwo Jima. Then the Vietnam veterans file past, some in wheel chairs, and we know again that war is not all glory. When the local priest gives an invocation at the reviewing stand, we feel his words resonate in our bones as he thanks God for peace and asks for continuing mercies. The sacred is very much in our midst. Those who have died, Warner would say, become powerful sacred symbols that organize, direct, and constantly revive the collective ideals of the community and the nation.

But is this a full picture of Memorial Day? Is this the prototype of public ritual, or is a different image better? Shift our attention from the small town to the massive gatherings at air force bases that have become the site of many contemporary Memorial Day festivities. Low over the trees from show left a squadron of four F-4 Phantom fighter jets thunders into view. Over the public address system the announcer explains to an assembled crowd of 500,000 that the squadron will form the "missing man" formation in honor of all those who have died in combat. As the planes pass directly across show center, the right wing plane accelerates at a ninety degree vertical angle and disappears with a roar into the clouds above. The symbolism is as powerful as the fighter's engines. In our minds we see the pilot's soul rising to be united with God.

In that brief moment we know that the sacred dimension of public ritual is by no means a thing of the past. Yet it is a brief moment. We do well to linger awhile to see what other glimpses of the sacred we may gain by the end of the day. Four hours pass. Almost forgotten is the missing man formation and the brief invocation given by a chaplain of unidentified faith who prays to the God of duty and freedom. Much more vivid in our minds are the skydiving team that unfurls a large U.S. flag at five thousand feet overhead; the simulated attack on an enemy air field, complete with real paratroopers and simulated cluster bombing by a B-52; a partial reenactment of the raid on Pearl Harbor, with aircraft reconditioned for the movie *Tora, Tora, Tora;* and a forty-five-minute precision flying demonstration by the Air Force F-16 Thunderbirds.

The event illustrates how much public rituals have departed from the small-town ceremonies Warner described half a century ago and how much the sacred values they express have also been altered. We see no faces and no wheel chairs; the human dimension is virtually absent. What impresses us most is the technology. Again and again the announcer tells us how much faster the planes of today fly than those of only a few years ago. Against such power, an enemy will likely be too confused and afraid to fight at all. The mock battle includes a token human element in the Green Berets, who appear like specks in the distance as they parachute from their open-sided Hueys. More impressive is the fact that the battle requires six fire trucks, four buses, three heavy-duty forklift tractors, and an eighteen-wheeler, besides all the fighter jets, helicopters, and transport planes. It is evident that such ceremonies are staged productions and that they symbolize the contributions of special groups to the wider community. But the staging is done for a mass audience of people who know nobody else, and it is not the makeshift work of local volunteers but the professional work of aviators, engineers, public relations advisers, recording artists, and moviemakers. The groups that contribute to our well-being are now Lockheed, Pratt-Whitney, and General Dynamics.

The Varieties of Public Ritual

The Warner-type rituals that take place in small towns and the air base spectacles that draw hundreds of thousands of spectators symbolize the two extremes of contemporary public ritual. The former are by no means defunct. They exist in the parades sponsored by volunteer fire companies, in the festivals put on by civic organizations to commemorate their villages' anniversaries, in the various ethnic fairs that draw idle suburbanites on hot summer afternoons, and in a host of other events, from 4-H fairs and Fourth of July celebrations, to craft and hobby shows, to flea markets and antique auctions. All these draw people from the wider community, not simply the members of a particular church or synagogue, and they dramatize certain collective values, such as community spirit, self-sacrifice, the importance of tradition, or simply having fun. At the other end of the spectrum, drawing much larger crowds and much greater media exposure, are such mass spectacles as Memorial Day air shows, the Macy's Thanksgiving Day parade, the Rose Parade on New Year's Day in Pasadena, numerous rock concerts and athletic events, and televised productions put on for mass audiences, ranging from presidential inaugurals, to the centennial anniversary of the Statue of Liberty, to such annual events as the Miss America Pageant and the Academy Awards. In between these two extremes is a wide variety of public rituals that draw larger and more diverse audiences than neighborhood ceremonies do but are not as massive and anonymous as those at the latter end of the spectrum. College and professional athletic events, for example, may draw audiences of ten to a hundred thousand and include much in the way of deep symbolism about loyalty, team work, and success. Political campaigns at the county, district, and state levels often provide an occasion for public rituals of similar magnitude. State fairs, such large metropolitan festivals as the St. Patrick's Day parades in New York and Boston or the Shriner's parade in Philadelphia, and the holiday and daily closing ceremonies at such theme parks as Disney World also illustrate the great variety of public rituals.

Scholars interested in the sacred have long been attracted to public rituals. These are among the most significant ways in which what has been called "civil religion" is produced. Civil religion, narrowly conceived, is the use of God language with reference to the nation. When the inscription on a coin reads "In God We Trust" or when we pledge allegiance to a nation that is "under God," we are engaging in the practice of civil religion. Presidential speeches that quote from the Bible or conclude with the phrase "God bless America," invocations at air shows or at sessions of Congress, and references in history books or at Fourth of July pageants to the divine covenant on which our nation was founded also illustrate this kind of civil religion. More broadly conceived, civil religion may be defined as the symbolism by which a people interprets its historical existence in light of transcendent reality. In this broader view secular myths that make no specific reference to the supernatural could also be considered part of the civil religion. Marx's vision of historical materialism, for example, has supplied a kind of civil religion for many communist regimes. In the United States and Western Europe a secular civil religion has long been constituted by concepts of natural law, fundamental human rights, principles of freedom and equality, and notions of civic virtue.

In both its broader and narrower constructions civil religion is of fundamental importance to any understanding of the public expression of the sacred. Civil religion embodies a society's sense of sacred time, giving it an understanding of its origins, the significant events in its past, and the direction of its movement through history. U.S. civil religion is rich with stories about its colonial origins, the heroic men and women who served their country in larger-than-life ways, the struggle for independence, the founding of a great nation, the expansion westward, the inclusion of immigrant populations, and its wars. Civil religion defines a nation's fundamental purposes as well. Whether these are conceived as the promotion of economic progress, the defense of the nation, or participation in foreign wars, they are always legitimated in terms of basic conceptions of transcendent reality. Ideas about God's will, about economic laws, or about fundamental human rights provide the language in which such projects are identified and defended. A civil religion also supplies the basic definition of who belongs to the nation and who does not. At one moment in history this definition may restrict full citizenship to white, male, property holders who are members in good standing of their churches. At another moment in history it may include all persons age eighteen or over who live within certain borders and can show certifiable proof of citizenship. In addition, a civil religion always helps identify a people by contrasting them with other groups and other values that are regarded negatively. Communism may be considered a fundamental evil to be avoided at all cost; others may take the same view of poverty, economic underdevelopment, or a lack of higher education and scientific advancement.

The civil religion is thus of fundamental importance to a society because it integrates an entire people, drawing them into a common circle of identity, giving them a shared language about a common heritage, and defining certain absolutes about which they can all agree. As such, civil religion always runs the danger of becoming self-worship or self-glorifying nationalism, as it does when a particular regime or policy is defended as an absolute, unquestionable good. But civil religion also contains a critical dimension, for in identifying a transcendent reality that is more basic than any action of the nation-state itself, civil religion allows specific plans and policies to be criticized. Raising questions about the morality of abortion laws in terms of scriptural teachings, or about defense policies in comparison with standards of peace and justice, illustrates how civil religion can be critical or prophetic rather than simply a means of legitimation.

For organized religious bodies, civil religion is likely to have both negative and positive consequences. The negative consequences are that universal, least-common-denominator values may replace the distinctive traditions of particular religious communions. For example, the civil religion may emphasize having faith in God but deny the need for salvation through Jesus Christ. More negatively, the civil religion may also substitute secular conceptions of the sacred for those associated with churches and synagogues by, for example, elevating faith in technology over faith in God. On the positive side, civil religion is one of the main ways in which religious bodies can influence the secular society and an important means by which they in turn gain legitimation. A religious organization concerned about the plight of the homeless, for example, may be barred constitutionally from engaging in direct political activities in behalf of this cause but can appeal to the conscience of voters and elected officials in terms of biblical conceptions of justice and equality that are built into the American civil religion. In return, religious organizations may gain added support for their own programs of worship and religious instruction when a political leader confers legitimacy on them by seeking God's blessing on the nation.

Because civil religion is composed of long-standing historical myths and because it often functions best by simply being taken for granted, it has been common to regard it simply as an element of a nation's culture — as a set of implicit values so deeply infused in every institution that it more or less maintains itself. Children learn about it from their parents and in their classrooms, and they continue to be exposed to it in subtle ways through its presence on coins and in speeches and books or when they sing the national anthem. But civil religion, like any other cultural element, is in fact produced. Resources, planning, time and effort, money, lobbying, legislation, and professional expertise are all required to maintain it. This is why public rituals are so important. They are not the only means of maintaining the civil religion, but they are clearly among the most significant. They are the occasions on which presidents invoke God's blessing or appeal to citizens to pass legislation in the name of scientific progress. They associate military technology with freedom in the minds of school children. They define character, beauty, athletic prowess, and personal success for millions of television viewers. They give parents the opportunity to discuss patriotism with their children and clergy the occasion to link national holidays with religious teachings in their sermons.

Social observers have in recent years paid increasing attention to public rituals of all kinds because these events provide important insights into the fundamental values of the society in which they occur. A society in which witches are periodically burned or drowned probably has different values from one in which more than a hundred million people sit glued to their television sets each January on a Sunday afternoon while two teams of highly paid athletes battle for a football championship. In many such rituals the name of God may be invoked, helping to associate the divine with other important values, but public rituals also help us understand the role of the divine by showing that secular values may be even more capable of generating collective enthusiasm than are those associated with the supernatural. It has thus been common for students of public rituals to adopt a functional definition of the sacred, regarding it as whatever emerges in the ritual as most deeply cherished and most fundamentally regarded as an absolute value. The focus of attention, then, is on the ways in which the ritual is constructed and the kinds of values and beliefs it reinforces, whether these be explicitly religious or functionally alternative conceptions of the sacred.

The examples that have been cited thus far suggest some of the important dimensions along which public rituals may vary. Size of audience, and implicitly of the community or public being represented, is a fundamental dimension of variation. As the two kinds of Memorial Day celebration indicate, other factors, such as the degree to which participants are known personally or whether sponsoring organizations are likely to be small voluntary associations rather than multinational corporations, are likely to vary along the same continuum. Just as we have discussed in the context of congregations, small public rituals are likely to involve people who are bound together by other social ties, such as family, community, or work attachments, whereas large rituals are likely to draw people who remain strangers to one another and have no other basis for interacting beyond viewing the ritual itself. Other dimensions of variation include the sponsorship under which the ritual occurs, ranging from churches or religious confederations, to secular community organizations in the voluntary sector, to those closely connected with the state (such as political rallies), to those sponsored by for-profit organizations (such as professional athletic teams, rock concert promoters, or theme parks). Both the nature of sponsorship and the degree of professionalism with which a public ritual is orchestrated bring us to the question of how these events secure resources from their host environments.

Rituals and Social Resources

Although public rituals appear on the surface to represent a different form of religious expression than those deriving from congregations, religious hierarchies, religious special interest groups, or academies in that the latter are all formally organized, it should be evident that public rituals are increasingly the product of specific organizations or clusters of organizations as well. In Warner's Yankee City case, the Memorial Day ceremonies involved weeks of planning by various voluntary and civic organizations. In the air show version of Memorial Day, thousands of troops are pressed into service to provide security, direct traffic, and perform other duties, and all are supervised by an officer and staff responsible for the entire operation. Other public rituals are no different. Small-scale events, such as a local fete put on as a hospital benefit, may involve a chair who serves as a full-time volunteer for much of a year and a large number of subchairs and committees. Large-scale events are more likely to be produced by some of the growing number of promotional firms that contract to organize all the festivity's aspects, from subcontracting with private security firms for their services, to making similar arrangements with catering firms, to working with theater companies and actors' guilds.

Most of us are probably aware of the extent to which public rituals involve organized effort. Whether one has served on a fete committee or has simply read about the enormous amount of money and professional expertise that goes into such events as the Rose Parade, beauty pageants, or the Olympics, it should be clear that rituals do not just happen. Yet it is important to stress that rituals are produced because this fact has often been neglected in scholarly discussions. One theoretical perspective suggests that rituals emerge spontaneously from social crises, thus denying the importance of organization and planning. A witch trial, for example, is said to happen because the community somehow feels itself under attack. That may be, but other studies of witch trials demonstrate the importance of church leaders in translating these feelings into action. A second theoretical perspective also ignores the planning that goes into public rituals because it focuses on what these rituals reflect about broader norms and values. In this view an adequate explanation of the Super Bowl would be that the American public values athletic competition. Clearly more is involved than this, though. Everyone values motherhood, but it took a presidential order and a vast greeting-card industry to turn Mother's Day into an important national ritual. In other cases money may not be so important, but contributions of time are of the essence.

One of the significant determinants of whether public rituals can be put on at all, and on what scale, is the ability of some group or organization to evoke voluntary commitment. Such commitment, it appears, depends largely on personal networks that create a sense of obligation to help out. One may be convinced that mental health, for example, is a worthy cause, but in the abstract one is more likely to send in a check than to devote time unless the person soliciting time happens to be a neighbor, a fellow church member, or a coworker. It is for this reason that most of the examples given thus far of public rituals in small towns involve voluntary effort. They can depend on such effort because of the ties that bind people together in these communities. In the absence of such ties, organizers who wish to put on public rituals must rely to a much greater extent on institutional resources and the marketplace. An air show, for example, can be staged largely without voluntary effort because tax monies can be funneled through the military to put on such events in the name of community relations and recruitment. Making sure that the event is sufficiently entertaining to draw large crowds also helps provide the necessary resources because concessionaires can be charged substantial fees, knowing that their profits will more than cover these costs.

In the past religious organizations were able to play a significant role in shaping public rituals because of the networks and commitments they reinforced at the personal level. Besides providing the Memorial Day sermons that Warner observed, local congregations were responsible for maintaining cemeteries and monuments, putting on funerals, building floats for parades of all kinds, sponsoring Boy Scout and Girl Scout troops, and enlisting volunteers in other community agencies. Should commitment to local congregations erode, either through a more privatized version of religious commitment or a general decline in volunteer effort, one of the casualties would be the ability of religious organizations to influence the character of public rituals. As for-profit firms enter the picture in increasing numbers, promoting public rituals for mass consumption, the ability of religious organizations to play an active role is also likely to diminish.

Public rituals are thus a particularly interesting means of expressing the sacred as far as religious organizations are concerned, not because they are unplanned or unorganized but because they remain one of the most powerful means of expressing the sacred, even though they are largely outside the control of established religious organizations. The messages that churches, religious hierarchies, and religious special interest groups try to communicate are at least initiated under their own auspices and can often be targeted toward a specific audience. Public rituals, on the other hand, seem increasingly to emanate from political or for-profit organizations, but they may still include references to God, prayers, or adaptations of religious narratives. These messages reach millions of people, yet they may leave much to be desired in the eyes of religious authorities, which may partly explain why some religious authorities challenge and counteract secular rituals.

That public rituals are, to a greater degree than other public expressions of the sacred, outside the control of religious organizations is, in at least one respect, positive for the character of a nation's civil religion and its confessional religious heritage. As we have seen in previous chapters, the need for religious organizations to perpetuate themselves has a decided influence on the kinds of ideology they project. It is easy, for example, for the public to hear a preacher talk about spreading the gospel and conclude that the preacher simply wants to build a larger church and advance his or her own career.

When religious language appears in public rituals not sponsored by any religious organization, it may well seem more spontaneous and genuine. A movie star who expresses thanks to God when receiving an Oscar, or a rock musician who asks a prayer for peace, may be much more compelling than a member of the clergy making the same statements. The negative side of using such words in secular contexts, of course, is that a wary public can also attribute cynical motives to the politicians or marketing people who have decided to include them. But it is the speaker rather than the entire religious message that becomes the focus of skepticism.

Their inability to control the religious content of public rituals is perhaps the key reason why clergy and other religious leaders are often unhappy with the quality of American civil religion. Fused with other messages, religious content in these settings is likely to be brief, formulaic, and on the surface superficial. Asking God to bless the nation can never substitute for the theologically informed instruction people receive in sermons and Sunday school classes. If religious organizations lack control, they nevertheless play a complementary role and indirectly influence the religious content of public rituals. A rock singer who includes a gospel tune in a public concert may do so because of religious training, and a president who asks God's blessing on the nation is likely to include this invocation because of regular interaction with members of the clergy. Religious leaders may occasionally lobby for certain kinds of prayers to be voiced or may influence public rituals directly (for example, by encouraging political leaders to observe a national day of prayer), but more likely their influence will be indirect.

Television and other communications technologies, from pay-per-view cable options to sound amplification systems, have had one of the most direct effects on public rituals. When the human voice could be heard by crowds no larger than a few thousand people, the odds were high that local community organizations would play an active role in producing public rituals. When satellite technology makes it possible for a single rock concert to be viewed live in countries all around the globe, these odds are greatly diminished, because organizations with command of the necessary professional expertise take over. It is no accident that the largest public rituals staged in recent years in behalf of various charitable causes, such as relief for victims of AIDS, have been sponsored by entertainers rather than churches. This is not to deny the continuing role of religious organizations in raising money for charitable purposes, the scale of which is far greater than that raised by an occasional relief concert, but it does point to the limits of religious organizations in promoting large public rituals.

What television has also encouraged, however, is the increasing commercialization of public rituals. When Lincoln gave his Gettysburg Address, a few enterprising individuals might have made money by selling lemonade to the crowd, but nothing can compare with the market forces prevailing on public rituals that depend on television advertising. In these rituals the fundamental elements of our civil religion may be preserved, at least when slogans about freedom are included and an occasional reference to Lincoln or Washington is made. These sacred values, however, cannot help being contaminated when Miller Lite intrudes every five minutes to sell good-times drinking at the beach. It is particularly hard to commemorate the deeper, more sober dimensions of our civil religion, such as the tragedy of lives lost in war or the suffering of innocent children, if public rituals have to sell entertainment to mass audiences.

Ritual Activity

Also shaping the content of public rituals are the standard activities of which they are composed. These activities have traditionally been heavy on the side of behavior or action, such as dances, gestures, and other performances, rather than verbal speech alone. Indeed, the first generation of social scientists who examined rituals, including Émile Durkheim and Bronislaw Malinowski, generally distinguished between ritual, which they saw as a kind of collective behavior, and belief, which they regarded as more purely cognitive and verbal. Ritual acted out the beliefs, and beliefs (or myths) explained what was going on in the ritual. The prototype of ritual was thus a tribal dance in which participants acted out a specified routine, each element of which was a behavioral symbol, an act that stood for something having a deeper meaning, because it corresponded to a specific belief. In contemporary settings a wedding would provide a clear example because each component of the ceremony, including such acts as the lighting of candles and such physical objects as the rings, conveys a symbolic meaning. In public life the coronation of the queen of England has been shown to follow this pattern, each component action demonstrating traditional understandings of the authority of the queen and her relations to the law and her subjects. A ritual can thus be understood as a set of activities that follow a formalized code or pattern to express symbolic meanings about social relations. Generally, public rituals are simply more formalized and elaborated versions of behaviors in ordinary life, such as tidying one's room or tipping one's hat, that also help align our relations with other people and with ourselves.

Because their meaning is so often encoded in activities rather than in words, public rituals must be examined with special attention to the form or staging that is involved. This is why an airplane's leaving its formation to disappear vertically into the clouds is a masterpiece of ritual drama. Even without interpretation a deeper meaning is communicated. Politicians know the importance of form and staging as well. When the president addresses the National Association of Religious Broadcasters, certain elements of the religious community receive a powerful boost, whether the president says anything encouraging or not. This is also the reason that implicit messages must be so carefully considered, whether they are planned or unintended. Forklifts and fire equipment may be part of the stage crew rather than the production itself, but they help communicate the importance of technology. A huge flag carried by skydivers is likely to make a much more memorable impression, even if nothing is said about it, than a carefully written opening prayer.

It is also important, though, to understand the verbal content associated with the behavioral form of public rituals. In the case of a primitive tribal dance nothing has to be verbalized because the community and its tradition are so tightly knit that everyone already knows what each specific action means. In modern contexts these understandings are not likely to be so well understood or so widely shared. People live in different subcultures and bring their own understandings as they view a public ritual. When these rituals invite viewers to look on merely as individual spectators, there will also be little interaction among them to help define the situation. One family attends an air show expecting to be entertained. Another attends as an act of remembrance. However symbolic the flight path of a particular airplane may be, it helps that the announcer has framed the event by describing it as a missing man formation.

In modern societies there is likely to be a complex mix of enacted and verbalized messages in public rituals. Unlike in the primitive case, verbal communication is needed to restrict the possible meanings an enacted event can convey, but unlike in the public rituals that arose during the age of oratory and still prevail in many Protestant religious services and academic halls, speech alone is seldom powerful enough to constitute an engaging public ritual. Television again is one of the reasons why. It has conditioned us to expect pictures of action as well as "talking heads." It has also made possible the mixing of speech and action. Other than the occasional comment provided by the announcer, for example, a professional football game viewed in person is mostly an enacted ritual. For the television viewer, however, it is as much verbal commentary as it is action. This is another reason why television has had such a profound impact on public rituals. It has the capacity not only to present the action but also to interpret that action.

The interplay between action and interpretation, however, also points to the importance of situating public rituals in a wider context. Although a Fourth of July celebration may be defined as a discrete event taking place, say, on the Mall in Washington, D.C., the ritual itself is actually part of a much wider complex of public interpretations and commentaries. Clearly the news media help frame the event, perhaps by featuring a small group of protesters who used the occasion to denounce recent government policies toward abortion, but religious leaders, academics, and writers also play an important role in defining the event's meaning to the public. Certainly this has been the case in major national events, such as space launches, inaugurations, presidential assassinations, civil rights marches, and antiwar demonstrations. Religious leaders especially need to be mindful of the role they can play in providing interpretations of such public rituals.

When verbal interpretation is supplied in the ritual itself, the activities of the ritual can be relatively diverse instead of having to follow the close conventions of a primitive dance. For example, spectators at a Phillies baseball game can suddenly find themselves subjected to a ceremony commemorating Benjamin Franklin's discovery of electricity. The announcer simply explains what is going on. Rituals are constrained, however, by the requirement of having to follow formalized rules and informal expectations to communicate successfully. Ben Franklin can be celebrated, for example, during the pregame show but not in the middle of an inning.

The fact that public rituals must follow certain conventions has important implications for understanding what they may communicate about explicit religious themes. Starting public events with a prayer is a long-standing expectation for many rituals that otherwise have no religious content at all. As long as this expectation holds, spectators will implicitly gain the impression that prayer is at least a part of the ordinary scheme of things. Prayer is, we might say, normalized by appearing at the start of athletic events, air shows, and meetings of Congress.

A second way that religious content benefits from the formal patterning of rituals derives from the fact that secular rituals sometimes make use of religious themes because these themes provide a familiar pattern to follow. The use of such patterns is often particularly evident in movie scripts and television shows that follow biblical episodes, such as the story of the Good Samaritan or the crucifixion and resurrection of Christ. Rock music patterned after gospel songs is another example on a smaller scale. Large public spectacles may also make use of religious patterns, such as modeling the sequence of events like that of a church service or following an enactment of evil, such as the bombing of Pearl Harbor, with a ritual of salvation, such as the aerial precision of F-16 fighters. Implicitly, the religious message may be reinforced by some of these adaptations, even though the explicit content is secular.

In a different way the activities involved in public rituals are likely to diminish their religious content, however. As wider and wider audiences have been sought, especially for rituals whose success depends on advertising and gate revenues, the level of professional specialization has increased. Quite apart from the mixing of commercial and more serious values that may occur, professionalization itself works against the inclusion of religious themes. At these events a local preacher may be asked to give an invocation, but it would be extremely unlikely for a church choir to be asked to sing the national anthem or the church softball team to perform during halftime. Religion is thus pushed toward the informal, local, amateur side of public life, while professional entertainers capture the stage at the national level. This is not to say that religion itself is unprofessional, but specialization encourages the public to think that religious professionals should be concerned with what happens in churches and synagogues and that public rituals are better handled by choreographers, actors, directors, and script writers.

Understanding the rising influence of professional specialization also helps us better understand the differentiation of audiences we have considered in several previous chapters. In the present context we might say that public rituals are increasingly defined for a mass, national, or universal audience, while religious services are associated with specialized, local, and particularistic audiences. Anyone—regardless of background, ethnic origin, or creed—should be able to appreciate the presidential inaugural or the Rose Parade, but we would not expect everyone to feel comfortable at the local Presbyterian church or to be happy listening to a television preacher speak out on national politics. The reason is partly because public rituals push religion into the category of amateurism. For mass audiences, we have been conditioned to want the most polished entertainment that professional specialists can provide. Apart from a few personalities, such as Billy Graham and the pope, religious actors have been unable to satisfy that demand.

Expressing the Sacred

These considerations suggest that the manner in which the sacred is expressed in modern public rituals will be influenced by (1) the availability of large organizations capable of sponsoring such rituals, (2) broad cultural values that will ensure a large audience for these rituals, and (3) form and content that follow certain expectations. For these reasons the sacred is more likely to be expressed through occasional references to the divine in otherwise secular rituals than in public rituals organized by religious bodies themselves and more likely through powerful secular images than in explicit religious language. Public rituals sponsored by local voluntary organizations will be more likely to retain such language, helping to constitute what some have described as a gulf between localism and cosmopolitanism or between folk culture and official culture. The public rituals that command the greatest media attention and the largest audiences are likely to express the sacred in different ways, though.

What renders the content of public rituals sacred in the first instance is the fact that these rituals are set off from ordinary life. Just as church services gain power from small rituals setting them off from weekday activities, public rituals are surrounded by similar distancing mechanisms. Many of them happen only on holidays; many of them occur only once a year; increasing numbers, such as sports events and beauty pageants, involve competitions that define the final episode as a very special occasion indeed. It is also difficult to think of major public rituals based on ordinary working activities. They are instead associated with nonwork life, particularly free time and entertainment.

A second factor that defines public rituals as sacred activity is their power to command large audiences. This power, as we have considered before, is not the decisive factor, but it is significant. There must be something special, we tell ourselves, about an event that can command millions of viewers or hundreds of thousands of spectators. We say this because we implicitly believe the ritual speaks to something primordial in human nature. When it attracts a wide audience, it in fact gains legitimacy from our conceptions of human nature.

Public rituals also convey a sense of the sacred because they evoke total commitment from their participants. In personal life we may be impressed that the supernatural really exists when we see somebody willing to die on the mission field to tell others what they believe. In public life we cannot help but take seriously something that others of our species have expended so much energy developing. Watching an athlete perform in the Super Bowl, we can say to ourselves, "That person could have retired and lived comfortably; this must really be important if they are willing to sustain injury and forego other pleasures for it." The competition built into public rituals, from sports to beauty contests to politics, simply enhances this means of expressing the sacred. Competition requires those who participate in public rituals to become better at what they do, to devote themselves totally to it, to struggle daily for the mental discipline such activities require.

The content—the values—that takes on sacred significance is shaped by the way in which these rituals produce and define the sacred. Human virtuosity, for example, is dramatized as a high value because of the discipline and talent it takes for people to participate in competitive public rituals. A professional football player may kneel in a brief prayer after scoring a touchdown, and a president-elect may give thanks to God for the victory, but the God being recognized is chiefly a God of human nature who bestows supreme talents on some individuals. It is not a God of mercy who accepts everyone no matter how badly they fail.

There is of course a lesson in this for the ways in which religious organizations might position themselves in relation to public rituals. One reason why religion has fallen into last place as a player in large public spectacles is that few people understand or respect the meaning of religious virtuosity. Mother Teresa is an exception because people can see she has devoted her entire life to activities they themselves could never perform. The pope is an exception of a different sort because he has at least worked his way up the ranks to become the head of a large multinational organization. But most other religious professionals are regarded as nice, trustworthy people you might like to have as friends but would never pay money to see perform.

Were the solution simply to establish stricter criteria of virtuosity for the religious life, religious organizations might do well to launch national and international competitions in which the most spiritual, the most peace-loving, the most well-versed in scripture could battle it out in an olympics of the soul. Clearly that solution would have huge negative effects, however, for spirituality has always been considered too mysterious to subject to precise rules of the game. Indeed, it may be far more effective for religious organizations to posture themselves as the antithesis of public rituals. Everybody may love a winner, but the number of losers will always be greater than the number of winners. Messages of hope, acceptance, forgiveness, and mercy will have a place, whether they gain the widest audience through public rituals or not.

It is nevertheless important to acknowledge the other values that are made sacred in public rituals. Some of these, like the quest for human greatness or the exaltation of self, may be fundamentally at odds with certain religious values, while others are neutral or benign. Science and technology, for example, have become greatly reinforced as sacred values through contemporary public rituals. From air shows to televised space launches to presidential speeches about the importance of mathematics in grade school, science and technology gain respect and urgency in the public mind. As a result, public opinion polls over the past few decades have shown growing numbers of people who think science can solve all our problems and declining numbers who think religion can.

Closely related to the idolization of science and technology is the faith in national economic and military power that many public rituals express. Freedom depends on having F-16s that can fly twice the speed of sound and perform 360-degree maneuvers in less than a quarter-mile radius. That freedom might depend on other things, such as character or civic virtue, is more difficult to convey in public rituals. Economic prowess is shown by the fact that we can build such jets or by the new automobiles we see on display at the shopping mall or by the president's state of the union address. These values are likely to pay little attention to the supernatural. If there is a God at all, it is a deity who blesses our efforts and ingenuity, not one who worries about tradition, the environment, or human community.

Human community, however, is a more complex value than are science and technology as far as religion is concerned. Public rituals do express community of a sort, and some versions of community have powerful religious undertones. When millions of people watch something on television, there is a sense of being in it together, even if they are all viewing separately. We feel we are Americans when we hear the national anthem sung at the Super Bowl. We also have something to talk about when our team wins or loses. In this sense public rituals help forge a national identity. Even advertising does this because we all know the same products and the same slogans. This is important. When social observers worry that the social fabric is unraveling, they need to remember that Mickey Mouse and Pepsi are part of our common culture, giving us symbols that define our heritage and holding us together in the same way that the flag and our common beliefs in God do.

Nevertheless, this sort of community is always problematic from a religious standpoint because the quality of our collective identity is also at stake. Community may be possible on the basis of self-interest alone, as we often assume on the basis of our indebtedness to Locke and Bentham. Or it may be possible through loyalty to a totalitarian leader, as Hitler hoped. But public rituals must be occasions for the expression of virtue as well as mere community. They must bring us together, not simply in our faith in high-speed aircraft but also in our desire to work for the good of our country. This is why precision flying is such an attractive feature of such rituals. It demonstrates the capabilities of the aircraft and, even more important, the training and dedication of the pilots.

Many of our public rituals do dramatize civic virtue as well as community based on self-interest and consumerism. Entertainers who put on performances to raise money for charitable causes may benefit in good publicity for themselves, but they also show that success and concern for the needy are not contradictory. They dramatize the value of charitable activities. Public rituals of many kinds also provide role models that demonstrate the importance of such long-standing values as hard work, discipline, commitment, and the use of one's talents. Even though these role models may not be known personally, they can have a powerful influence in directing energies toward positive ends.

Religious leaders are likely to find some of these role models neutral insofar as they endorse nothing worse than hard work and dedication. In other cases public rituals have provided the occasion for religious leaders to capitalize on the publicity of such role models, pointing out that they are also good Christians or activists for peace or whatever. If religious organizations are generally excluded from formal participation in public rituals, this at least is a way that the religious community can interact with those in the limelight.

Challenges and Prospects

The most serious challenge that has generally been identified in discussions of public rituals is the breakdown of community in modern societies. With fewer people living in small towns like the one Warner studied, public rituals may be impossible to mobilize and may not be able to affirm common values when people are utterly absorbed with their own lives or when the society is composed of such diverse elements. That has been the fear, but the examples we have been considering suggest otherwise. The transition from traditional to modern social arrangements has not so much diminished the importance of public rituals as it has altered their form. Local community rituals have not died out, anymore than local religious services or pick-up basketball teams and high school plays have, but superimposed on top of these local rituals are large spectacles that would not have been possible before the advent of sound amplification and television technologies.

The impact of mass communication on public rituals appears to be much the same as its effects on athletic events. Despite fears that telecasts of these events would erode actual attendance, people still flock to televised athletic events of all kinds. Television has, however, altered the character of these events by, for example, requiring more time outs and providing instant replay possibilities. The same is true of public rituals. Nationally televised events help create a national culture—small children know vastly more about the life of their president than ever before; people of all ages can engage in casual conversation about a popular actor or singer. Even the most trivial elements of this national culture play a vital role in sustaining the civil religion because they provide conversation starters, an initial basis of trust, and common metaphors. At the same time, mass communication has not replaced the public rituals that draw people out of their homes to participate in community events. People still turn out to see an Independence Day fireworks display or a small band of Cub Scouts parading down the street. Mass communication does, however, affect the content of these local rituals as well. Speeches may be less common because television has conditioned us to want action more than words alone; the characters riding on floats may be suggestive of Disney cartoons; politicians may turn up hoping to be featured on evening newscasts. Religious leaders have probably thought little about these influences. Public rituals will continue, yet the effects of mass communications may provide opportunities as well as limitations for the public expression of religion.

Another challenge, more potential than actual as yet, is the weakening of organized religion. Should spirituality become more private or invisible, what would the consequences be for public ritual? Many theoretical arguments suggest that public ritual would not diminish as a result but that its content would change. It would not diminish because there seems to be a need in all societies for such events. This is not to say that the need is rooted in deep psychological structures. But institutions appear to have a social need to engage in ritual activity. Governments seem to survive better when they are able to communicate their accomplishments, and business firms find it in their interest to stage company picnics or sponsor floats in the Rose Parade. In Western European societies, such as Germany and

Sweden, where religious organizations are much weaker than in the United States, public rituals still abound, but the Social Democratic Party may be the sponsor rather than the local alliance of churches.

The weakening of organized religion would alter the content of public rituals simply because even the most taken-for-granted themes in these rituals are constantly open for negotiation. Constitutional separation of church and state in the United States has encouraged the formation of special interest groups concerned with excluding all manifestations of religion in the public arena. Business interests are often convinced that religion is such a divisive issue that it is better left alone. As a result, it is certainly imaginable that references to God would gradually cease to be part of public rituals were it not for the presence, both organized and individual, of spirituality among community leaders and in the wider society.

More challenging than the erosion of religious influences in absolute terms, however, is their erosion relative to the increased role of the nation-state. One of the ways the federal government has enormously expanded its reach into the daily lives of the average citizen is through its ability to orchestrate massive public rituals. The Nazi rallies organized by Hitler provided the first evidence of the importance of such rituals in modern societies. Democratic societies have seldom tolerated the self-display or the expense associated with rallies of that kind. Yet the fiscal power of the nation-state, both to command tax revenues and to evoke voluntary contributions from the private sector, has made it possible for central regimes to organize public rituals on a more frequent basis and larger scale than ever before. Within the past two decades, for example, officials of the U.S. government have bombarded the American public with a nearly continuous series of events celebrating the national bicentennial, the bicentennial of the Constitution, the bicentennial of the Bill of Rights, the centennial of the Statue of Liberty, and the victory by U.S. troops against Iraq, as well as much-expanded presidential inaugural ceremonies every four years. In addition, public officials have appeared more frequently than ever before on television, not only to give speeches but also to make guest appearances in honor of retiring actors, to attend award ceremonies, and to add luster to such televised Hollywood galas as the fiftieth anniversary of the USO.

The danger of this increased ritual activity on the part of the government is that civil religion gradually turns into self-congratulating, politically expedient nationalism. Freedom and patriotism may still be championed as fundamental values, but so are glitz, smooth talking, and the ability to appear well-dressed and successful in public. Humility is more difficult to display on such occasions. Mercy, forgiveness, and justice are also difficult concepts to portray before an audience of Hollywood celebrities. Having captured the public stage, political leaders can also use these events to argue for their own programs, turning a university commencement address into a platform for berating the opposition. Critics feeling the need to lift a prophetic voice against regime policies are likely to be at a considerable disadvantage.

Many observers have recognized the danger that civil religion will become nationalism under these conditions, but fewer have been mindful of the equally serious challenges to public ritual that have arisen as a result of the emphasis on materialism in contemporary culture. The problem is not, as advertisers sometimes like to suggest, that individuals are simply so oriented toward material things that they want their public rituals to be flashy and filled with expensive things to buy. Rather, as we have seen earlier, it is more a function of the ways in which public rituals are produced. Relying less on volunteer labor and more on professional expertise and attempting to reach wider audiences by using television, public rituals become major economic endeavors. Advertising becomes more important, as does the sponsorship of large corporations. In the process religious messages are likely to be deemphasized relative to those of technology and consumerism.

Innovation in public ritual, therefore, most likely will come from the state and market sectors and will depend on profitability and the development of new technologies. Religious organizations will need to seize whatever opportunities that may become available as well. But it also seems likely that the role of religion will become more indirect and that religious leaders can make the greatest use of public rituals by interpreting them and using them as illustrations for their own purposes. Certainly public rituals will continue to provide common experiences toward which religious leaders can address their own perspectives.

The greatest need will be to find ways to infuse values of meekness and mercy, peace and justice, and a concern for the oppressed and the voiceless into the public arena. Religious organizations must not succumb to the pressures of the marketplace in seeking ways to do this. Nor is public ritual the only way in which these values can be expressed. The examples of Mother Teresa, various relief efforts, and even some figures in secular life suggest that there may be creative ways of keeping these values alive despite the wider cultural forces that are reshaping the character of public rituals.

Conclusion

The presence of religious values in the public arena is not something to be taken for granted. These values are there because of the conscientious efforts of thousands and thousands of people who believe their own lives and that of the whole nation are better when matters of faith and conviction are given free expression. They are there not simply because these individuals happen to believe in God, pray, meditate, and try to live out their spirituality in their private lives. As we have seen, public religion is produced—it is the product of a complex system of organizations that expend resources to bring the sacred into a relationship with the social environment.

The Role of Communities

In some other time or place we would have found it necessary to emphasize the role of communities much more than we have in this volume in order to understand how public religion is produced. Communities are the natural social entities in which people live— their neighborhoods, villages, extended families, and ethnic groups. Throughout most of history communities have been the roots from which religious conviction has grown. At the end of the Middle Ages in western Europe virtually the entire population was divided into small communities of no more than several hundred people, who lived within walking distance of a local chapel and could generally organize their day around its rituals. As recently as a century ago most Americans lived in either small farming communities or ethnic enclaves in the cities. Limits in transportation technology kept them from straying too far from their neighborhoods; friends and extended families made these communities supportive settings in which to live. The sacred played an integral role, manifesting itself in the family devotions that might have been heard in a neighborhood of Scottish Presbyterians, at the daily morning mass attended by Irish Catholics, or in a Sunday evening hymn sing at the Baptist church.

The role of traditional communities such as these in promulgating public religion should not be underemphasized. Even today many of these communities occupy a powerful place in the lives of those who have grown up in them. Polish and Lithuanian Catholics still cluster in neighborhoods where the church is a dominant social institution. Black churches reach perhaps a larger share of their surrounding neighborhoods than any other community organization does. Uprooted rural southerners and midwesterners find new friends by gravitating toward Baptist churches in the suburbs of major cities. Without these indigenous communities that link the sacred to the food, the smells, the clothing, and the customs that are so deeply ingrained in childhood memories, public religion would have little lasting power at all.

Yet it is formal organizations that must be emphasized if we are to grasp the ways in which public religion is actually perpetuated. The public arena in modern societies is not just an assemblage of private individuals who come out once in awhile to vote or who register their opinions on social issues by talking to a Gallup pollster on the telephone, spending the rest of their time in the family room watching television. The public arena is much more aptly described as a highly organized social environment in which the key players include banks and labor unions, international firms, marketing agencies, television networks, huge nonprofit organizations, telephone and transportation systems, and an endless variety of government bureaus, law offices, military installations, prisons, hospitals, colleges and universities, and schools. Religion may be a matter of the heart, a supplement to the family, a solace for the lonely, but it would scarcely have the public influence it does if it too did not operate as a vast system of complex organizations.

Complex Organizations

The presenting face of American religion is its congregations — the local churches, parishes, synagogues, fellowship halls, chapels, and even mosques that can be found in virtually any location. Despite their familiarity, these are perhaps the most deceptive of all religious institutions, for they refer to themselves as communities and try to cultivate an atmosphere of collegiality and informality, yet they are formal organizations through and through. Behind the seeming ease with which a pastor's sermon is delivered lie committee meetings, telephone calls, budgets and financial reports, and plans for everything from church growth campaigns to the supervision of janitorial services. The so-called megachurches that sport memberships in the thousands are especially likely to function in this manner, employing highly skilled managers to oversee their multimillion-dollar budgets, but even the proverbial "little brown church in the vale" is likely to have a far more complex organizational structure than meets the eye.

In an earlier time, when hamburgers were still being served up at the local mom and pop cafe, most churches were already a part of vast franchise operations that would put McDonalds to shame. These denominational hierarchies helped decide where new churches should be located, supplied them with interim financial aid and a temporary pastor, sent in teams of lay administrators from sibling organizations to set up the necessary charters and bylaws and to negotiate with planning boards and zoning officials, and made sure the whole operation became self-sufficient within a few years. In return these outposts of the soul sent back a portion of their income to denominational headquarters, paying for staff members to start additional churches, print educational materials, utter public statements on social issues, and file briefs on behalf of various court cases and legislative actions. As the McDonalds of the world became better organized on a national scale, these hierarchies were well placed to exercise their voice in the public square.

When other organizations found it advantageous to specialize, religious communities followed suit. That one chain sold round hamburgers while another sold square ones was far less important than the fact that fast-food industry as a whole was establishing its own charities, educational foundations, training institutes, lobbyists, health professionals, and liaisons with advertisers, meat packers, and environmentalists. In a world filled with specialized interest groups of all kinds, religious organizations have adapted quickly to make their own interests known. Many of these, as we have seen, resemble secular political action committees, functioning mainly to lobby on Capitol Hill for one issue or another, to bring legal action to bear if necessary to champion these causes, and to mobilize the dollars and sensibilities of the wider population. Religious special interest groups have also proliferated to take the place of more traditional communities, giving lobbyists ways to be in touch with others of similar convictions, helping isolated individuals with painful addictions to find support, or providing clergy with insurance, reading material, new ideas, and professional conferences.

In an environment that so greatly values higher education, colleges and universities have emerged as yet another important vehicle by which religious values are created and disseminated to the wider public. With culture as their principal stock and trade, these organizations have been able to fill in many of the gaps left by the traditional congregational mode of operation and the newer special interest groups. Church-related colleges and universities have declined in importance relative to secular institutions of higher learning. Many church-related institutions still provide attractive alternatives to public higher education, however, and at secular colleges and universities ideas about religion are produced on a large scale in a number of disciplines, are communicated to large numbers of students, and are supplemented through the work of campus ministries, chaplaincies, and various student organizations.

We have also considered the extent to which public rituals—the occasions on which so many sacred ideals have been communicated in the past—have become spectacles orchestrated by large configurations of government agencies, entertainment companies, and marketing firms. If the decline of community relative to formal organizations is evident within the religious realm itself, it is certainly evident here. Although many of these spectacles pay homage to the divine in some way, they more compellingly communicate that what really holds the public sphere together is the genius of technology and entrepreneurship. Public rituals demonstrate clearly that the government funds, concessionaires, and media rights from which monies are derived to pay for such spectacles have deep implications for the content of the sacred in public life.

The various kinds of organizations we have considered play complementary roles. There is, in social science parlance, a "division of labor" among them that reduces some of the competition that might otherwise prevail and ensures more religious representation in the public arena than there would be if only one kind of organization were present. The particular strength of congregations lies in their ability to include whole families (and especially children), promote interaction among families, and mobilize sentiment at the local level. Religious hierarchies complement the work of congregations by coordinating activities requiring a broader geographic framework or more substantial funds than any single church or synagogue could generate. Special interest groups can also mobilize resources on a larger scale, but they add flexibility beyond what religious hierarchies can generally provide by focusing on single issues or causes. Colleges and universities are exceptional arrangements for securing the resources necessary for scholars to engage full-time in the production of knowledge and for these ideas to be instilled in the malleable minds of young adults. Public rituals complement these other means of expressing the sacred by linking basic social values with the media and with large crowds on occasions of special importance to the life of the society itself.

Paying the Piper

Although these various organizations fill special roles, they are all subject to common pressures and constraints. None of these organizations is prevented from producing expressions of the sacred that can be communicated in the public arena, but all of them are constrained to speak in certain languages and to say some things rather than others. These same constraints, however, also make it possible for the sacred to be produced in the first place. As is true with any of the resources that we depend on as individuals, common currencies pay the piper but also pick the tune.

The public sphere remains vibrant in the United States because constitutional provisions restrain the hand of government, the free enterprise system and government agencies play roles that often neutralize the power of the other, and a strong network of voluntary associations is in place that enjoys a high degree of autonomy from the for-profit sector and the political sector. Religious organizations compose a significant part of this voluntary sector. In many other advanced industrial societies the public sphere is much less vital because government has been more effective in orchestrating major social functions, the free enterprise system is more closely supervised by government, and the nonprofit sector is much narrower. In these societies religion is more likely to be aligned with government as well, leaving it less latitude in criticizing official policies and making it less attractive to the wider citizenry as an alternative to the political system. If religious leaders contribute to the public sphere at all, they do so behind the scenes by conversing with political authorities, or they act quietly and safely to support government programs or oppose them only in symbolic ways.

The dynamism of the public sphere in the United States contributes positively to the functioning of all the kinds of religious organizations we have considered. Congregations have never been supported officially by public monies the way they have been in Europe, and governments have generally been reluctant to regulate the activities of local churches as closely as they have other nonprofit and for-profit organizations. Congregations have thus been able to appeal in good faith to individuals' voluntary giving, claiming rightly that these donations are all that stand between them and failure. Fears of the possibility of government restriction, combined with substantial independence from government, has made it possible for congregational leaders to criticize the political system from a wide variety of positions, ranging from the extreme right to the extreme left. Denominational hierarchies have enjoyed much the same freedom. They have always been constrained in their public statements by the beliefs of powerful constituents at the grass-roots level, but this constraint is quite different from the top-down limitations that prevail when denominations are supported by government. Special interest groups have also enjoyed this freedom. Although somewhat more limited because of their overt partisan efforts, they still benefit from a political system that provides motivation to speak out on public issues and an economic system that provides ample funds from which these groups can draw. Colleges and universities are in a somewhat different position since they are so heavily dependent on public monies for their operations, yet special provisions deriving from norms of academic freedom and pertaining to other nonprofit organizations as well give these institutions wide latitude in contributing to the nation's public culture. Public rituals, as we have seen, may enjoy the least autonomy from the political system because they are often orchestrated by political officials themselves, but these rituals also flourish because of the enormous economic resources on which they can draw. In each case, then, religious organizations benefit from the social norms that restrain government intervention, from the material affluence of the for-profit sector, and from the organizational models, legal arrangements, and cooperative relations that prevail in the broader nonprofit sector.

The U.S. public sector also influences the public activities in which religious organizations engage, though. Until half a century ago, the federal government was so inconsequential at the local level that congregations seldom paid any attention to it at all, unless there was a war or religion became an issue in presidential or congressional elections. In the last few decades, however, the role of the central government has grown so substantially that all kinds of religious organizations have been forced to pay greater attention to it. In so doing, they have inadvertently contributed to the perception that *government* and *public* are synonymous. To influence collective values, organizations now feel compelled to work through the various branches of government, whereas in earlier times they were much more likely to exercise influence on values through preaching itself, training children, and supporting family relationships. In focusing so much attention on political activities, religious organizations have also blinded themselves to the influences of the economic sphere. One might expect to hear discussions in adult Sunday school classes of church-and-state relations, but lessons on "church and capitalism" would seem out of place. The influences attributable to the church's dependence on the free enterprise system are nevertheless manifold. They range from a reluctance to speak out against the pressures of the capitalist system itself, to a feeling that the realities of economics are simply beyond comprehension by religious people, to outright materialism, careerism, and greed in pulpit and pew. Even the well-oiled mechanisms of the nonprofit sector have not been an unmitigated blessing for the churches. The social welfare services provided by secular nonprofit agencies have often outstripped the work of religious organizations, causing many people to believe true caring is less likely to come from religious sources than from humanitarian values. Secular nonprofits not only compete directly with religious organizations for contributions but also channel different messages into the public arena. In recent years, for example, secular nonprofits have made such a virtue of program effectiveness and the good feelings that come from caring for others that religious organizations have sometimes jumped on the same bandwagon instead of retaining the spiritual basis for their appeals.

An emphasis on program effectiveness is but one of the implicit cultural norms that pervades the public arena because it is so heavily dependent on complex formal organizations. Whether political, economic, or charitable, whether secular or religious, formal organizations operate according to bureaucratic norms that not only help them convey substantive messages in the public arena but also become part of the message itself. Rationality is one of the underlying assumptions on which these organizations are based. Were it not for this assumption, planning could not occur, vast programs could not be coordinated, and personnel could not be counted on to carry out these programs. Rationality itself may not conflict with the deeper spiritual orientations valued by religious organizations, yet it does preclude or marginalize much of what religion has stood for throughout the centuries, and it conflicts with other values and worldviews only partly because of the ways in which bureaucracies actually operate. Although there is much in these organizations that defies rationality, the important cultural message is that these organizations are carefully planned and controlled, with someone in charge at all times who arranges the most efficient means to accomplish clearly specified ends. People associated with these organizations must play "as if" games to convince themselves that everything is functioning according to rational logic. Clergy may thus believe in divine intervention in human affairs, but they must plan their building programs and pledge drives as if no such intervention were likely. The physicians who sit in their congregations may believe in miraculous cures, but the hospitals at which they work provide little room for these cures to be recognized.

It is perhaps for this reason that an entire underground of alternative institutions exists besides the ones we have been considering—institutions ranging from seance parlors to psychic healers and from astrologers to mystics and mental health gurus, all of which point to the possibility of a reality other than the one institutionalized in the major organizations of the dominant society. These alternative institutions focus much more on the private lives of individuals than on the public discourse of the nation itself, but the line separating the two is never absolute.

The overweening reliance on rationality, means-ends efficiency, and formal propriety by established religious organizations also provides a clue to understanding the continuing appeal of religious orientations that consciously distance themselves from some of these dominant norms. Jehovah's Witnesses, for example, pride themselves on violating the respect for private space that is so much a part of an individualistic, anonymous, mass society. Most established religious organizations abide by norms of civility, which prevent them from intruding on any of the political, economic, or leisure activities dominating the daily lives of ordinary individuals. Jehovah's Witnesses violate these norms because they regard them as secondary to the higher principles they see in their scriptures. The fortitude to run amuck of these social conventions must evoke a certain degree of admiration from anyone who understands the arbitrariness of these conventions. More generally, the appeal of fundamentalist religious groups is that they provide an alternative perspective, a counter-discourse, to the safe, respectable, predictable, rational worldview of dominant religious organizations. Fundamentalists hold forth the possibility that the course of history does not depend ultimately on these organizations but is directly in the hands of God, who may intervene at any time. If the center of the public arena is influenced by a rationally constructed religious discourse, then, there is always a peripheral counterdiscourse (constructed by an alternate rationality) that lurks in the woods just beyond the clearing, sending forth signals about a world inhabited by miraculous, demonic, and angelic forces.

The public sphere in the United States is also in constant flux, and some of the dominant developments appear likely to alter the role that even the most powerful religious organizations can play in the future. If there has been a linear trend toward greater government centralization and control of the public sphere, this trend has nevertheless been accomplished in fits and spurts. With two dominant political parties, three major branches of federal government, and a multiplicity of state, regional, and local jurisdictions, government agencies themselves have competed to provide new services or to woo taxpayers by promising to curtail these services. Had

some political mastermind merely imposed a fifty-year plan on the
nation in which each new governmental activity was preordained,
the churches might have reluctantly played along and turned their
attention to other activities. Since each new proposal is contested
in the political realm, however, religious leaders have felt a moral
obligation—and an opportunity—to debate these proposals. Much
the same sort of uncertainty in the economic realm has contributed
to the vibrancy of religion's role in the public arena. Years of economic prosperity have made it possible for denominations to launch
building programs and add staff interested in various causes. Years of
economic retrenchment have often hit religious organizations especially hard, forcing them to look harder at auxiliary programs, pare
down to what are perceived as essentials, and perhaps devote more
of their resources to the unemployed and the homeless. The overall complexity of the social environment at any given point is thus
amplified by the changes to which religious organizations are exposed over time. The uncertainty accompanying these changes is
conducive to added variety in the religious realm.

Public and Private

It is evident from all this that religious organizations do contribute
actively to the production of public values. These organizations may
be constrained to follow certain procedural norms as they try to influence the public sphere, but influence it they do. The sacred and its
various implications are brought into the public square in hundreds
of thousands of sermons and Sunday school lessons, in the social
statements issued by denominational leaders, through the lobbying
of special interest groups, by college professors and campus minis-
ters, and in the rituals enacted on national holidays. Yet the question
remains, how closely are these public manifestations connected with
the private religiosity that really matters to individuals themselves?

The relation between public and private religion is best considered at the congregational level, for it is here that a close relation
has most often been assumed to exist. The pastor preaches a sermon
that influences the private beliefs of those who listen, and the lis-
teners in turn encourage the pastor to speak more of the same, and
they put their dollars in the offering plate to help make this pos-

sible. The only problem with this cozy relationship is that it seldom exists so neatly in practice. Most congregations hide an enormous range of private religious views. When parishioners are questioned individually about their beliefs, they admit to having idiosyncratic notions about central tenets of the faith, combine snippets of theology from the various churches they have attended or books they have read, and weave everything together in a pattern that reflects their own personal experiences more than anything they have ever heard articulated in public. They feel this is the way faith should be — a matter of personal exploration and groping, not a subscription to a predigested set of doctrines. They may also feel their beliefs are so personal that it is inappropriate to share them at all, especially if sharing leads to unsettling disagreements. In a climate like this, how can there really be a public spirituality at all?

A possible answer to this question is suggested by what social scientists have called "intersubjectivity." The sort of private or internal spirituality just described would be an example of a subjective belief or orientation — something quite shielded from public view, quite internal to the individual's own consciousness. A sermon text, in contrast, would be an example of an objective cultural artifact — something external to the speaker, an object, a tangible product that people can view or hear or touch, discuss, and agree at least about its existence. In between these presumably lies something that people do not necessarily talk about and may not be able to see or touch but nevertheless share. The statement " 'up' is toward the sky" might be an example. An assumption of this kind is intersubjective because everyone seems to agree about it, even though they do not discuss it. We may know from science courses that "up" is an arbitrary physical designation, but we feel secure in our private sense of vertical direction because everyone else seems to be making the same assumption.

Intersubjectivity is a convenient idea because it suggests both the importance of community and the way in which something private may be linked to the wider public. Community is important because it is through observing other people's behavior that we are able to confirm the "sharedness" of our subjective assumptions. When we see other people standing up or lying down, for example, we draw certain inferences about the meaning of *up*. Were we to think about it harder, we would also realize that definitions of *up* remain unspoken most of the time, yet our private assumptions about this term are very frequently reinforced by public pronouncements. When the announcer on the evening news says the stock market went "up," we see an arrow pointing in a certain direction, or when we see on television that the air force sent "up" a spy satellite, we may also see a picture of something rising into the sky.

Analogous arguments can be made about intersubjectivity as the vital connection between private spirituality and public religion. There may be a strong norm against sharing our most intimate thoughts about the divine, so we sit quietly in church and never say anything to our neighbor in the pew beside us. Yet we assume that we are both there for the same reason. Our copresence reinforces our private belief. Community is in this sense important. Our very presence also makes public our private convictions. It dramatizes or enacts the subjective, making it objective. The process is no different from the ones that take place in other sectors of a highly individuated society. When peasants worked together as a whole community, tilling the same fields, their subjective definition of the situation could easily be reinforced by actual talking about the weather, how the crops were growing, and so on. Later, when farmers tilled their individual fields, talking was much diminished, and the definition of work became much more internal or subjective; nevertheless, farmers could look across the fence, see that their neighbor was doing similar things, and thus assume intersubjectively that there was a common bond, a similar understanding of the world, that they shared with their neighbor.

We know intuitively, however, that something is wrong with this analogy when it is applied to contemporary religion. The person in the pew may be comforted at one level by seeing another person sitting quietly, appearing to be praying, or participating in the same service of bread and wine. "This is a fellow believer" may be the obvious conclusion. At another level, though, we know enough of what is going on to ask ourselves, "Is this person even worshipping the same God? Are we really fellow believers, or are we here for quite different reasons?" This is the consequence of spirituality's having become so deeply attached to the subjective consciousness of the individual that everyone's convictions can be different from everyone else's. Spirituality is in this respect not like tilling a field at all. Seeing someone hoeing a row of corn may provide us with strong clues as to what is going on; seeing someone sitting with eyes closed in a prayerful attitude provides only the vaguest clue about that person's spiritual life.

Intersubjectivity therefore provides only a tenuous thread between private and public religion. That our neighbor is sitting there at all is public testimony to the value of religion in a general sense, but we cannot assume that any of us believe exactly the same way or that we necessarily are lending our quiet assent to the public words being spoken by the minister. Our silent testimony contributes only to the implicit agreement that we have all decided to be there in the same place, that we have all decided to keep silent, and that we agree with "something" being said in public, perhaps some sort of core value or basic teaching about the importance of God. This is precious little on which to build the vast edifice of social pronouncements and programs we call public religion.

To understand why public religion is as strong as it is, we must seek an answer in something other than the idea of intersubjectivity. Part of the answer of course is that it may not make any difference what people really believe as long as they pay the piper. Perhaps people are there simply for show or because it is the thing to do in their community, but they put in their check, which allows the church to run its programs, send money up the hierarchy, operate special interest groups, and the like. From a purely organizational perspective, we might conclude that public religion operates entirely at the public level, soliciting support by making people feel good or by putting on church suppers that have very little to do with public religion at all. To argue this, however, would not only be overly cynical but also miss something vital about public religion itself.

Public religion is powerful because it creates its own connection with the ostensible spirituality of private individuals. It does so not in the silent ways suggested by the idea of intersubjectivity but through the language constituting public religion itself. Public religion, like private religion, is essentially a language of tradition, of narrative, and of conviction. It may be promulgated by large impersonal organizations, but for it to be effective these are the dimensions of genre that it must embody.

Tradition is important because it links specific values or contemporary policy statements to a long history of cultural wisdom. For the individual, spirituality is likely to be framed in terms of personal tradition—in the past most often through stories of family heritage and in the present through the language of personal journeys, development, and spiritual discovery. For public religion, it is the wisdom of the ages that still counts. For believers themselves, God is understood to be a creature of revelation that acts in and through history. For outsiders, the faith is still a matter of collective tradition, the highest truths forged in the long evolutionary history of a people. It may have to be presented as part of a particular "communion" or "confession," but that is not to diminish its value. The very organizations that promulgate it have legitimacy by virtue of their history, their investment in the perpetuation of a collective memory, and their procedures for applying traditional wisdom to changing circumstances. Despite all its efforts to be rational and effective and to follow the same norms that other bureaucracies do, the church is what it is because it upholds a faith *tradition*.

Narrative is the language of choice for public religion. When individuals speak about their deepest spiritual insights, they tell stories. When religious organizations try to do the same, they also need to use the language of stories. Other languages are often used as well of course; for example, the church has a long history of borrowing the language of the state, of law, and of scientific academies to frame logical arguments about particular theological positions. Narrative, however, remains the code of choice for a variety of reasons. Its fundamental characteristic is the unfolding of events according to a temporal sequence. Narrative is thus especially well suited for connecting moral prescriptions with tradition. Narrative also tends to be self contained; it employs a high degree of intratextuality or self-referencing. As such it is not easily disconfirmed by outside events or alternative stories. Understanding the narrative requires the listener to enter into its own internal logic. Narrative also invites this sort of identification between the listener and characters in the story. Whether there is true intersubjectivity between the subject and the text or not, the text suggests there is.

Conviction must also be a feature of public religion. Most people can appreciate private spirituality that is held deeply; they cannot appreciate hypocrisy, fickleness, or insincerity. For public religion to carry weight, it must also be presented as a matter not just of the head but of the heart. Narrative is again the language of choice for doing this because it requires a speaker, an authorial voice, and it can either place the speaker in that voice or give it to a character who speaks authoritatively. The story allows characters to reveal a connection between their own internal feelings and their more rationally derived conclusions. It also puts the speaker in a setting in which these connections can more easily be understood. It is little wonder advertisers have found mininarratives the best way to sell their products. Preachers do the same when they speak from personal experience. They bring a private element, a sense of conviction, into the public arena.

As this allusion to advertisers suggests, large bureaucratic organizations can certainly produce cultural artifacts that bear the mark of sincere personal narratives. As we have also seen, however, there is an inherent tension between the implicit messages that large organizations necessarily give off and the explicit messages they try to present to the public. A television preacher may be able to "speak candidly from the bottom of my heart" about a public issue, but this statement may be less credible to those who know it was developed by Madison Avenue professionals and brings in thousands of dollars that help pay loans on a luxurious office building. It is perhaps even more problematic, however, for religious organizations to abandon the special genre best suited to their message, opting instead for the dry verbiage of legislative bills and academic monographs. The strength of congregations remains the heartfelt sermons preached regularly, not the mission statements and bylaws they produce to legitimate themselves to the state. Religious hierarchies, special interest groups, and academics may contribute indirectly to public religion by making it possible for preachers to preach or by working behind the scenes to produce position papers, legal briefs, or academic studies, but they can also continue to have a direct role in the production of public religion if they retain the languages of tradition, narrative, and conviction.

Discourse about Public Religion

We come then to a final issue: the relationship between discussions of public religion and public religion itself. If public religion works best when it is true to its own genre, we must ask whether it is strengthened or diminished by being analyzed and discussed in terms other than these. The question is perhaps like one that prevails in literary circles: does good literature benefit from literary criticism, or does literary criticism detract from good literature?

We can answer this question best not by jumping to a hasty defense of literary criticism and its analogous disciplines but by considering the limitations inherent in public religion as we have just described it. If public religion speaks best with reference to particular traditions, these traditions are necessarily limited in their appeal because people in contemporary society hale from a great variety of traditions, seldom have a deep knowledge of any of these traditions, and are likely to have drunk so deeply from the well of progress that tradition itself may have negative connotations. If narrative is the language of choice, its value is still only poorly understood. Scientists also rely heavily on narratives, for example, but the public assumes science is a different language, the hallmark of which is mathematics, not fairy tales and folklore. People who work closely with politicians know that nothing is so likely to move them as a compelling personal story, yet there is also a widespread perception that politics is a world of dry legal argumentation. Conviction too is limited because contemporary culture imposes strong norms of detachment and objectivity on public behavior. We may know that doctors and lawyers are convinced of the high prestige of their professions, but we want them to act as if they were not, taking everything in stride, showing no emotion, keeping a cool head about the business at hand.

These limitations may reflect misunderstandings of the importance of tradition, narrative, and conviction, yet they are genuine restrictions on the character of public religion itself. A public religion that reflects no consensus in the body politic but is a mere assemblage of competing subcultures can scarcely be powerful in setting societal goals. Nor can a public religion be powerful if it is regarded as mere storytelling or special pleading. Useful as these languages may be, a complex and heterogeneous society also requires metalanguages that can bridge particular traditions, particular stories, and particular convictions. This is the role that discourse *about* public religion can play.

Talking about public religion rather than the language of public religion itself helps us, just as literary criticism does literature, to appreciate why it works, why it is meaningful to us, and how it can be more effective. We can stand apart from our separate traditions long enough to reflect dispassionately on those traditions, perhaps coming to a greater appreciation of the role of tradition itself. Talking about public religion provides a vantage point from which to bridge subcultures. Only when that happens can genuine consensus be forged. Metadiscourse allows us to appreciate why stories are important, what is common to all our stories, and what is distinctive in each story. Being able to talk about our convictions, as well as simply expressing them, allows us to see that they are convictions, helps us to detach momentarily from them, and encourages us to find a language that does not close the possibility of others' revealing their own convictions.

Pluralism has always been a vital feature of American public religion. As the extent of this pluralism increases to embrace new religious traditions, new interest groups, and even new definitions of the sacred, it will be all the more valuable — and difficult — to maintain. A vast array of organizations is in place to carry out the task. These organizations must learn to talk dispassionately about their various religious convictions, standing back from the traditions they represent long enough to see more clearly the convictions that others hold deeply. At the same time they must also remain true to the languages — of tradition, narrative, and conviction — in which public religion itself is best expressed. Only by doing both can they contribute to a broad understanding of the plural yet consensual manifestations of the sacred on which a vibrant society is based.

Further Reading

Introduction

For a rich conceptual and historical overview of public religion, see John F. Wilson, *Public Religion in American Culture* (Philadelphia: Temple University Press, 1979). An extensive bibliography dealing with various aspects of public religion throughout American history is provided in *Church and State in America*, 2 vols., edited by John F. Wilson (New York: Greenwood Press, 1986–87). Among the numerous works that examine religion's role in American politics, see especially the historical essays in *Religion and American Politics: From the Colonial Period to the 1980s*, edited by Mark A. Noll (New York: Oxford University Press, 1990); the broad overview in A. James Reichley, *Religion in American Public Life* (Washington, D.C.: Brookings Institution, 1985); the strategic issues addressed in *Government Intervention in Religious Affairs*, edited by Dean M. Kelley (New York: Pilgrim Press, 1982); and the nuanced empirical evidence in Allen D. Hertske, *Representing God in Washington* (Nashville: University of Tennessee Press, 1988), and in Peter L. Benson and Dorothy L. Williams, *Religion on Capitol Hill* (San Francisco: Harper and Row, 1982). For further theoretical background, empirical information, and international comparisons on the relations between religion, the voluntary sector, and the political and economic sectors, see the essays in *Between States and Markets: The Voluntary Sector in Comparative Perspective*, edited by Robert Wuthnow (Princeton, N.J.: Princeton University Press, 1991). On religion and the historic development of public space in democratic societies, see Max L. Stackhouse, "Religion and the Social Space for Voluntary Institutions," in *Faith and Philanthropy in America: Exploring the Role of Religion in America's Voluntary Sector*, edited by Robert Wuthnow and Virginia A. Hodgkinson (San Francisco: Jossey-Bass, 1990). One of the pleas for religious organizations to take a more active role in the public sphere that has been especially influential is Richard John Neuhaus, *The Naked Public Square: Religion and Democracy in America* (Grand Rapids, Mich.: William B. Eerdmans, 1984). Background on changes in American religion and its public role can be found in Robert Wuthnow, *The Restructuring of American Religion: Society and Faith since World War II* (Princeton, N.J.: Princeton University Press, 1988), and Robert Wuthnow, *The Struggle for America's Soul: Evangelicals, Liberals, and Secularism* (Grand Rapids, Mich.: William B. Eerdmans, 1989). Essential background on the broader tensions between private commitments and public responsibilities in American culture is given in Robert N. Bellah, Richard Madsen, William M. Sullivan, Ann Swidler, and Steven M. Tipton, *Habits of the Heart: Individualism and Commitment in American Life* (Berkeley: University of California Press, 1985). Theoretical perspective on the nature, development, and precariousness of the public sphere in modern societies is provided in Jürgen Habermas, *Legitimation Crisis* (Boston: Beacon, 1975), and Jürgen Habermas, *The Structural Transformation of the Public Sphere* (Cambridge, Mass.: MIT Press, 1990). There has been relatively little attention to reconceptualizing patterns of religious organizations in the way they are presented in the present volume; for an overview of the conventional approach, which focuses on church, sect, denomination, and cult distinctions, see Keith A. Roberts, *Religion in Sociological Perspective*, 2d ed. (Belmont, Calif.: Wadsworth, 1990), especially chapter 9.

Chapter 1: Cultural Production

An early volume that contributed greatly to defining cultural production as a distinct approach in the social sciences is *The Production of Culture*, edited by Richard A. Peterson (Beverly Hills, Calif.: Sage, 1976). A brief but more recent overview of developments in this approach is presented in Richard A. Peterson, "Symbols and Social Life: The Growth of Cultural Studies," *Contemporary Sociology* 19 (July 1990), 498–500. For a literature review that contrasts the cultural production perspective with other approaches, see Robert Wuthnow and Marsha Witten, "New Directions in the Study of

Culture," *Annual Review of Sociology* 14 (1988), 49–67. See also the entire issue of *Social Research* 45 (June 1978). Applications of this perspective to particular kinds of culture, which also provide broader insights, include Wendy Griswold, *Renaissance Revivals: City Comedy and Revenge Tragedy in the London Theatre, 1576–1980* (Chicago: University of Chicago Press, 1986), a study that particularly emphasizes the relations between cultural producers and consumers; Priscilla Clark, *Literary France: The Making of a Culture* (Berkeley: University of California Press, 1987); Alvin Kernan, *Printing Technology, Letters and Samuel Johnson* (Princeton, N.J.: Princeton University Press, 1987), which provides an excellent discussion of the role of market relations in cultural production and dissemination; Paul Hirsch, *The Structure of the Popular Music Industry* (Ann Arbor: University of Michigan Press, 1970); Howard Becker, *Art Worlds* (Berkeley: University of California Press, 1982); and Robert Wuthnow, *Communities of Discourse: Ideology and Social Structure in the Reformation, the Enlightenment, and European Socialism* (Cambridge, Mass.: Harvard University Press, 1989). *Vocabularies of Public Life: Empirical Essays in Symbolic Structure*, edited by Robert Wuthnow (London: Routledge, 1991), includes essays on the content of public discourse —religious, scientific, expressive, and policy—which emphasize the influences on this content of various cultural producers. On organizations and environments, especially the process of selective adaptation, see Robert Wuthnow, *Meaning and Moral Order: Explorations in Cultural Analysis* (Berkeley: University of California Press, 1987). On the role of organizations in institutionalizing ideas, see Mary Douglas, *How Institutions Think* (Syracuse, N.Y.: Syracuse University Press, 1986). The concept of isomorphism is amply developed in George M. Thomas, *Revivalism and Cultural Change: Christianity, Nation Building, and the Market in the Nineteenth-Century United States* (Chicago: University of Chicago Press, 1989); see also John W. Meyer and Brian Rowan, "Institutionalized Organizations: Formal Structure as Myth and Ceremony," in *Organizational Environments: Ritual and Rationality*, edited by J. W. Meyer and W. R. Scott (Beverly Hills, Calif.: Sage, 1983), 71–97, for a provocative discussion of the ways in which organizations adopt similar structures to legitimate themselves. On cultural exclusion, see especially Pierre Bourdieu, *Distinction* (Cambridge, Mass.: Harvard University Press, 1984), and Lawrence W. Levine, *Highbrow, Lowbrow: The Emergence of Cul-*

tural Hierarchy in America (Cambridge, Mass.: Harvard University Press, 1988).

Chapter 2: Congregations

A number of valuable ethnographies of congregations are available; see, for example, Nancy T. Ammerman, *Bible Believers: Fundamentalists in the Modern World* (New Brunswick, N.J.: Rutgers University Press, 1987), for a study of a conservative Baptist congregation; R. Stephen Warner, *New Wine in Old Wineskins* (Berkeley: University of California Press, 1988), for a fascinating ethnographic account of a Presbyterian congregation experiencing change over a two-decade period; Lynn Davidman, *Tradition in a Rootless World* (Berkeley: University of California Press, 1991), for a study of Orthodox Judaism that pays special attention to the role of women in congregations; and Albion M. Urdank, *Religion and Society in a Cotswold Vale: Nailsworth, Gloucestershire, 1780–1865* (Berkeley: University of California Press, 1990), for a rich contrasting case representing a different culture and period. Insight into specific characteristics of congregations, such as leadership, self-image, and education, as well as an overview of current congregational studies is provided in *Carriers of Faith: Lessons from Congregational Studies*, edited by Carl S. Dudley, Jackson W. Carroll, and James P. Wind (Louisville, Ky.: Westminster/John Knox, 1991). See also several of the essays on specific Presbyterian congregations in *The Mainstream Protestant "Decline": The Presbyterian Pattern*, edited by Milton J. Coalter, John M. Mulder, and Louis B. Weeks (Louisville, Ky.: Westminster/John Knox, 1991). Additional bibliographic materials and research suggestions are provided in *Handbook for Congregational Studies*, edited by Jackson W. Carroll, Carl S. Dudley, and William McKinney (Nashville, Tenn.: Abingdon Press, 1986). A historical study providing valuable insight into the ways in which religious ideas may be shaped by changing relationships between pastors, their superiors, and congregants is David Zaret, *The Heavenly Contract: Ideology and Organization in Pre-Revolutionary Puritanism* (Chicago: University of Chicago Press, 1985). Dean M. Kelley, *Why Conservative Churches Are Growing* (New York: Harper and Row, 1972), is still an exceptionally valuable treatment of the dynamics functioning chiefly at the congregational level. A study that provides historical background and some statistical information on black churches at the congregational level is C. Eric Lincoln and Lawrence H. Mamiya, *The Black Church in the African American Experience* (Durham, N.C.: Duke University Press, 1990). On church finances and volunteering of time, see *Faith and Philanthropy*, edited by Robert Wuthnow and Virginia A. Hodgkinson (San Francisco: Jossey-Bass, 1990). Especially valuable on the role of collective memory in congregations is James F. Hopewell, *Congregation: Stories and Structures*, edited by Barbara G. Wheeler (Philadelphia: Fortress Press, 1987). The discussion in the chapter that utilizes Durkheimian conceptions of the sacred draws especially on Émile Durkheim, *The Elementary Forms of the Religious Life* (New York: Free Press, 1967 [1915]). Older studies of congregations that are still useful for understanding the challenges facing particular kinds of churches include Walter Kloetzli, *The City Church—Death or Renewal: A Study of Eight Urban Lutheran Churches* (Philadelphia: Muhlenberg Press, 1961); Donald L. Metz, *New Congregations: Security and Mission in Conflict* (Philadelphia: Westminster Press, 1967); Oliver Read Whitley, *The Church: Mirror or Window? Images of the Church in American Society* (St. Louis: Bethany Press, 1969); and Gibson Winter, *The Suburban Captivity of the Churches* (Garden City, N.Y.: Doubleday, 1961).

Chapter 3: Hierarchies

There have been relatively few studies of denominational hierarchies, adjudicatories, and other church bureaucracies, although at this writing several important ones are in progress. One of the best studies to date of the ways in which positions in church bureaucracies influence the ideas and policies projected by those agencies is Gene Burns, *The Frontiers of Catholicism: The Politics of Ideology in a Liberal World* (Berkeley: University of California Press, 1992). A classic study emphasizing points of conflict between clergy or other denominational officers and local laity is Jeffrey K. Hadden, *The Gathering Storm in the Churches* (Garden City, N.Y.: Doubleday, 1969). Another classic study that deals specifically with the issue of centralization and decentralization is Paul M. Harrison, *Authority and Power in a Free Church Tradition: A Social Case Study of the*

American Baptist Convention (Princeton, N.J.: Princeton University Press, 1959). On the historical factors operating for and against centralization in American churches during the early national period, see Nathan O. Hatch, *The Democratization of American Christianity* (New Haven, Conn.: Yale University Press, 1989). Studies that provide insight into the hierarchical structures of specific denominations and confessional traditions include *A Case Study of Mainstream Protestantism: The Disciples' Relation to American Culture, 1880–1989*, edited by D. Newell Williams (Grand Rapids, Mich.: William B. Eerdmans, 1991); *American Denominational Organization: A Sociological View*, edited by Ross P. Sherer (Pasadena, Calif.: William Carey Library, 1980); and John D. Donovan, "The American Catholic Hierarchy: A Social Profile," *American Catholic Sociological Review* 19 (1958), 98–122. Studies of the roles and reward structures among church bureaucrats include Robert W. Peterson and Richard A. Schoenherr, "Organizational Status Attainment of Religious Professionals," *Social Forces* 56 (1978), 794–822; Thomas R. O'Donovan and Arthur X. Deegan, "Some Career Determinants of Church Executives," *Sociology and Social Research* 48 (1963), 58–68; Thomas R. O'Donovan and Arthur X. Deegan, "A Comparative Study of the Orientations of a Selected Group of Church Executives," *Sociology and Social Research* 48 (1964), 330–39; John A. Struzzo, "Professionalism and the Resolution of Authority Conflicts among the Catholic Clergy," *Sociological Analysis* 31 (1970), 92–106; and Charles H. Page, "Bureaucracy and the Liberal Church," *Review of Religion* 16 (1952), 137–50. On the implications of changing clergy employment patterns, see Robert L. Bonn and Ruth T. Doyle, "Secularly Employed Clergy," *Journal for the Scientific Study of Religion* 13 (1974), 325–43.

Chapter 4: Special Interests

The literature on special interests in religion is relatively sparse except for the spate of studies that have appeared in recent years on the Moral Majority and other organizations representing the religious right. My own discussion of "special purpose groups," their history, and their contemporary functions, including some empirical evidence, is in *The Restructuring of American Religion* (Princeton, N.J.: Princeton University Press, 1988), chapter 5. Discussions that focus on the issues advanced by some of these groups but also pay some attention to the characteristics of the groups themselves include James Davison Hunter, *Culture Wars: The Struggle to Define America* (New York: Basic Books, 1991), and Allen D. Hertske, *Representing God in Washington* (Nashville: University of Tennessee Press, 1988). Special purpose groups identified with the religious right, such as Moral Majority and Christian Voice, have received considerable attention; see, for example, the essays in *The New Christian Right: Mobilization and Legitimation*, edited by Robert C. Liebman and Robert Wuthnow (New York: Aldine, 1983), and *New Christian Politics*, edited by David G. Bromley and Anson D. Shupe, Jr. (Macon, Ga.: Mercer University Press, 1984). A classic study that should be read for background is James L. Adams, *The Growing Church Lobby in Washington* (Grand Rapids, Mich.: William B. Eerdmans, 1951). Studies focusing on other special purpose groups include Henry Clark, "The National Council of Churches' Commission on Religion and Race: A Case Study of Religion in Social Change," in *American Mosaic: Social Patterns of Religion in the United States*, edited by Phillip E. Hammond and Benton Johnson (New York: Random House, 1970); and Peter L. Benson and Dorothy L. Williams, *Religion on Capitol Hill* (San Francisco: Harper and Row, 1982).

Chapter 5: Academies

Studies of the religious role of colleges and universities are again attracting interest after a relatively long period in which this topic received little attention. At this writing, a major historical study of the ways in which colleges and universities have become secularized is under way by George Marsden at the University of Notre Dame, and a multivolume project focusing primarily on the changing character of church-related higher education is being sponsored by the Lilly Endowment. Several classic studies are still worth consulting for general background on the ways in which colleges and universities have contributed to the religious life of the United States: Merrimon Cuninggim, *The College Seeks Religion* (New Haven, Conn.: Yale University Press, 1947); Manning M. Pattillo and Donald M. Mackenzie, *Church-Sponsored Higher Education in the United States* (Washington, D.C.: American Council on Education, 1966); and Kenneth Underwood, *The Church, the University, and Social Policy* (Middletown, Conn.: Wesleyan University Press, 1969). Studies that provide helpful evidence on the role of academies of higher learning in particular religious traditions include James John Annarelli, *Academic Freedom and Catholic Higher Education* (New York: Greenwood Press, 1987); Andrew M. Greeley, *From Backwater to Mainstream: A Profile of Catholic Education* (New York: McGraw-Hill, 1969); H. George Anderson, "Lutheran Higher Education's Place among American Independent Colleges," *Susquehanna University Studies* 12 (1984), 33–44; *Church-Related Higher Education*, edited by Robert R. Parsonage (Valley Forge, Pa.: Judson Press, 1978); and William J. Byron, "Identity and Purpose in Church-Related Higher Education," *Susquehanna University Studies* 12 (1984), 21–29. For general overviews of the nature, culture, and social structure of American higher education, see *The Academic Profession: National, Disciplinary, and Institutional Settings*, edited by Burton R. Clark (Berkeley: University of California Press, 1987); Martin J. Finkelstein, *The American Academic Profession: A Synthesis of Social Scientific Inquiry since World War II* (Columbus: Ohio State University Press, 1984); Everett Carll Ladd, Jr., and Seymour M. Lipset, *The Divided Academy* (New York: McGraw-Hill, 1975); and Ernest L. Boyer, *College: The Undergraduate Experience in America* (New York: Harper and Row, 1987). Especially valuable on the relations between higher education and the social environment is Hardin Best, "The Revolution of Markets and Management: Toward a History of American Higher Education since 1945," *History of Education Quarterly* 28 (1988), 177–89.

Chapter 6: Public Ritual

Much of the literature on civil religion falls squarely into the category of public rituals insofar as civil religion is reinforced by inaugural addresses and national celebrations as much as, or more than, by religious organizations; see Robert N. Bellah, "Civil Religion in America," *Daedalus* 96 (Winter 1967), 1–21; Robert N. Bellah, *The Broken Covenant* (New York: Seabury, 1975); Robert N. Bellah and Phillip E. Hammond, *Varieties of Civil Religion* (San Francisco: Harper and Row, 1980); and Gail Gehrig, *American Civil Religion: An Assessment* (Storrs, Conn.: Society for the Scientific Study of Religion, 1981), for an extensive bibliography on the subject. On rituals and ceremonies themselves, see Conrad Cherry, "American Sacred Ceremonies," in *American Mosaic: Social Patterns of Religion in the United States*, edited by Phillip E. Hammond and Benton Johnson (New York: Random House, 1970); Victor Turner, *The Ritual Process: Structure and Antistructure* (Ithaca, N.Y.: Cornell University Press, 1969); and Robert Wuthnow, *Meaning and Moral Order: Explorations in Cultural Analysis* (Berkeley: University of California Press, 1987), chapter 4. The material on Memorial Day celebrations mentioned in the text is from W. Lloyd Warner, *The Family of God: A Symbolic Study of Christian Life in America* (New Haven, Conn.: Yale University Press, 1961).

Conclusion

Among the topics frequently referred to in the present volume but not examined systematically is the role of the mass media. Books examining the relationships between religion and the media include *American Evangelicals and the Mass Media*, edited by Quentin J. Schultze (Grand Rapids, Mich.: Academie Books, 1990); Jeffrey K. Hadden and Charles E. Swann, *Prime Time Preachers* (Reading, Mass.: Addison-Wesley, 1981); William F. Fore, *Television and Religion* (Minneapolis, Minn.: Augsburg, 1987); Peter Horsfield, *Religious Television: The American Experience* (London: Longman, 1984); Razelle Frankl, *Televangelism: The Marketing of Popular Religion* (Carbondale: Southern Illinois University Press, 1987); Stewart Hoover, *Mass Media Religion: The Social Sources of the Electronic Church* (Beverly Hills, Calif.: Sage, 1988); *Religious Television: Controversies and Conclusions*, edited by Robert Abelman and Stewart Hoover (Norwood, N.J.: Ablex, 1990); Martin E. Marty, *Improper Opinion: Mass Media and the Christian Faith* (Philadelphia: Westminster Press, 1961); *The Bible and Popular Culture in America*, edited by Allene Stuart Phy (Philadelphia: Fortress Press, 1985); and William Thorn, *Electronic Media Access in the 1980s* (Washington, D.C.: United States Catholic Conference, 1983). For an annotated bibliography that consists largely of articles in religious periodicals with special emphasis on media and evangelization, see *Christian Communication: A Bibliographical Survey*, edited by Paul A. Soukup (New York: Greenwood

Press, 1989), especially chapter 7. My discussion of the relation between public religion and private religion in this chapter is a more general treatment of the topic that follows some of the arguments initially developed concerning this relation in the context of religious television; see my *Struggle for America's Soul* (Grand Rapids, Mich.: William B. Eerdmans, 1989), chapter 6. On fundamentalism as a counterdiscourse, see especially the essays on Christian fundamentalism in *Accounting for Fundamentalisms*, edited by Martin E. Marty and R. Scott Appleby (Chicago: University of Chicago Press, 1994).

Index

ROBERT WUTHNOW is the Gerhard R. Andlinger Professor of Social Sciences and director of the Center for the Study of American Religion at Princeton University. He is a frequent contributor to scholarly and popular journals on American religion and cultural sociology. His eleven previous books include *The Restructuring of American Religion: Society and Faith since World War II* (1988), *The Struggle for America's Soul: Evangelicals, Liberals, and Secularism* (1989), *Acts of Compassion: Caring for Others and Helping Ourselves* (1991), *Rediscovering the Sacred* (1992), and *Christianity in the Twenty-first Century* (1993).

DATE DUE